A Heart of Excellence

A Heart of Excellence

How to Succeed at
What Matters Most
Physically, Emotionally,
Relationally and Spiritually

Laurie Ellsworth

HORIZON BOOKS
CAMP HILL, PENNSYLVANIA

HORIZON BOOKS
a division of
Christian Publications, Inc.
3825 Hartzdale Drive
Camp Hill, PA 17011
www.cpi-horizon.com
www.christianpublications.com

Faithful, biblical publishing since 1883

A Heart of Excellence
ISBN: 0-88965-186-8

LOC Control Number: 00-136394

© 2001 by Christian Publications

All rights reserved
Printed in the United States of America

01 02 03 04 05   5 4 3 2 1

Unless otherwise indicated, Scripture taken from
the Holy Bible: New International Version ®.
© 1973, 1978, 1984 by the International Bible Society.
Used by permission of Zondervan Bible Publishers.

To my loving husband, Mike

Your gentle spirit and wonderful sense of humor keep my heart healthy beyond measure.

Contents

Foreword... ix

Acknowledgments................................. xi

Introduction: A Matter of the Heart 1

Part 1: Relational

1 Friendship: Heart to Heart 7

2 Marriage: One Heart 37

3 Parenting: A Heart's Legacy 69

Part 2: Emotional

4 Stress: Soothing an Overburdened Heart 103

5 Stress II: Persuading Your Heart to Relax 131

6 Jealousy: Conquering a Heart That Divides 147

Part 3: Physical

7 Nutrition: A Heart Full of Energy................... 163

8 Exercise: Developing the Heart Muscle 185

Part 4: *Spiritual*

9 Faith: With the Heart of a Father 207

10 Discipline: Following Wholeheartedly 217

Recommended Reading 237

Foreword

It is my belief that as Christians we should strive to be our best, to be more disciplined than the rest of the world, to take better care of ourselves—after all, we represent the King! Whether personal or professional, at home, in ministry or in business, we need to have a heart of excellence.

That is why I connected immediately with Laurie when I met her at a CLASSeminar I was leading in 1996 in Kansas City. Our hearts beat as one. We were soul sisters. It was immediately clear that she had a heart fully devoted to the pursuit of godly excellence. A passion for truth and love, for helping those with burdened hearts, clearly burned within her. She spoke with boldness and unwavering confidence about the hope inside, and I found her enthusiasm and joy contagious.

In this book, *A Heart of Excellence,* Laurie reveals this passion that we share: how to pursue a heart that is fully devoted to what matters most.

Through her honest vulnerability, the strengths and weaknesses of her own heart, Laurie will draw you in. Her wisdom and practical ideas will give you a clear plan for how to maximize your priorities, your time and your decisions. Do you wish you could have more energy to get through the day? Do you long to get rid of anger and worry? Could you use more peace and less stress in your life? Are you eager to build relationships that don't crumble at the first sign of conflict? Do you wonder how to approach a perfect God?

If you answered yes to any of those questions, you are reading the right book! If you long for your life to reflect the very best that is in you, then allow yourself to embrace these pages. Read, highlight, reflect, jot notes on the pages, answer the discussion questions, apply, apply, apply. Then be ready for others to notice, for when we pursue excellence in what matters most it is always contagious!

Marita Littauer
President, CLASServices, Inc.
Speaker/Author of *You've Got What It Takes*,
Come As You Are and *Personality Puzzle*

Acknowledgments

Every book is a combined effort of many people. I would like to acknowledge the following people for their contributions:

George McPeek, you were the first to believe in the vision of this book and how it could impact the lives of others. I feel honored to be associated with such a kind and editorial director.

Janet Dixon, what a privilege it's been to work with you these past months. Your editing expertise was apparent from day one (when you sent me a four-page list of changes!). You were right every time and you consistently communicated your ideas with encouragement and humor.

Florence and Marita Littauer, your professionalism in our industry is a shining example to us all. You're known all over the world for you accomplishments in writing and speaking, and I'm humbled by the fact that you would invest yourselves in teaching and mentoring those of us just beginning.

Randy and Sarah Boltinghouse, every Sunday you bring us a glimpse of God's grace and mercy. Thank you for pastoring our church family with your God-given talent and love.

M*ike,* you are a gift straight from heaven. You've always encouraged me to pursue my dreams, but none of them could ever match what I've found in your love.

Above all else, guard your heart,
for it is the wellspring of life.

Proverbs 4:23

Introduction

A Matter of the Heart

As a personal trainer, I can analyze the strength of a person's heart by testing it. When Judy, a recent client, wanted to know how fit her heart was, I had her perform a test by walking or running on a mile-and-a-half course as fast as she could with an all-out effort. Judy had been exercising regularly, taking good care of herself and was injury-free. She huffed and puffed all the way, sweating after only a few minutes, but was able to push herself to the end without stopping. She finished in twelve minutes, which indicates a superb level of heart condition. She was all smiles when I congratulated her for developing such an excellent heart muscle.

For those who are unprepared for the test, it is not a pretty sight. Their exercise regime has been sporadic (or nonexistent). They've developed detrimental habits such as overeating, being sedentary, smoking, etc., to deal with stress, and they would probably rather have a root canal than try to pass this test. I stay beside them to monitor their progress and encourage their effort, but they are usually miserable. They may have to stop several times. Some bend over to rest their hands on their knees as they try to catch their breath. Some apologize; others plead, "Lord, just take me now!" Needless to say, their test scores indicate a less-than-fit heart, and they are usually embarrassed and ashamed that they have been less than excellent with its care.

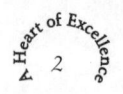

The condition of your heart matters! It's the primo muscle in your body. Numero uno. The head honcho. It has complete control. Like a dictator, it determines whether you live or die, whether you live a life of comfort—enjoying each day to the fullest—or merely struggle to get by. Without its cooperation, the rest of your body is rendered helpless. It is the first organ to function and the last to give up.

Small wonder it has so much power when you consider the magnitude of it. It weighs, on average, only about eleven ounces, yet it is forceful enough to beat 100,000 times a day, pumping 2,000 gallons of blood through 60,000 miles of cardiovascular system!

It is certainly worthy of respect and great care, yet study after study shows that most of us give it neither. Heart disease is still the number one killer in America, claiming over a million lives each year! I know firsthand the sting of those statistics. My father suffered his first heart attack at age forty-seven and his third at age fifty-two. Trust me when I say that nothing about heart disease is pleasant or joyful. It is a thief. It steals our joy, our health, our money, and it devours the short time we have together here on earth. It is a needless tragedy, but it is not an inevitable one.

There is much we can do to ward off heart disease with a healthy lifestyle and wise choices. We can make a difference in the kind of life we live (and sometimes how long we live) by focusing on simple daily activities that reflect and promote excellence.

This book has been created for just that purpose—to save lives! It combines the latest fitness research from credible sources, easy menus and meal planning and offers safe and helpful tips for making your health and energy soar. But *A Heart of Excellence* doesn't stop there. It combines mind, body and soul for a complete heart checkup.

Several months ago during my annual physical, I asked my doctor if he thought his patients (he has over 3,000) were becoming healthier since there has been such a tremendous emphasis on fitness in the last fifteen years. Without hesitation, he replied, "People are much more aware of what they should be doing—exercising, eating right, drinking more water, etc.—but they are not consistent. What concerns me even more is the shift I've seen in emotional and relational health. It's not good, not good at all. There is more family conflict, more divorce, more behavioral problems with children, more anger, more depression. Honestly, I find it startling that people who live in the greatest country in the world have so much pain."

It appears that the heart needs more than physical conditioning. It also needs comfort. It needs to be healed from relational wounds and scars from the past. It needs emotional rehabilitation. It needs perfect love.

The heart is the center of all we think, feel and do. It creates our motives, affections, passions and actions. It is the origin of all thought processes. Even Leonardo da Vinci, after dissecting the human body to illustrate it more accurately, said, "The tears come from the heart, not from the brain."

We cannot be completely healthy and whole until we focus on every aspect of the heart: relationally—are we taking care of our friends, children, spouse, parents with excellence? Do we allow ourselves the luxury of nurturing and being nurtured? Emotionally—do we understand what sets us off and what we can do about it? Physically—how are we taking care of the body God calls His temple? And lastly and most importantly, spiritually—do we know God and how to pursue Him?

Yes, I can test the strength of your heart physically, but every day the soul of your heart is tested by living with imperfect people. The outcome? Your character. Is it one that will allow you to stay the course, huffing and puffing at times, but reflecting all the good choices you made along the way? Will you be congratulated that you developed such a loving character, or will you have one that's weak and needy and not a pretty sight? You don't have to be embarrassed or ashamed by who you are. Conditioning your character is easier than you might think. It's a matter of the heart.

PART 1

RELATIONAL

Chapter 1

Friendship: Heart to Heart

Everyone's life is made more complete by the presence of a good friend. When we have someone we trust and delight in spending time with, our lives are enriched and we flourish in other areas of our lives as well. Friends recharge our emotional batteries and know how to encourage us and affirm our feelings. They are comfortable in the friendship and feel the freedom to be honest.

If a good friend tells us we have broccoli in our teeth, we take no offense and even thank them. They know what makes us tick and what makes us ticked, and they thoughtfully avoid the latter. They make the hard times bearable and the fun times memorable. Acceptance flows generously. They know us and believe in us so much that even when we have made a fool of ourselves, they do not feel that we have done a permanent job. Now *that* is a true friend.

Kathy and Julie are two of my friends who have proven their friendship is not fair-weathered, but true and strong. We met at church when our youngest children were just babies and found that we had many common interests. We were all full-time homemakers with a passion for God, our families and taking care of our health (eating right and exercising).

For several years while we all lived in the same town, we spent countless hours at the park playing in the sand with our kids, walking on trails or jogging through our neighborhoods for exercise, attending Bible studies together, exchanging recipes, planning cookouts, all the while talking and sharing our lives heart to heart.

But, as you can imagine when you spend a significant amount of time with people, all was not Camelot. There were fights between our children to be mended, thoughtless words to be forgiven and major differences of opinion to be accepted. But through all that, and maybe even because of those difficult times, we developed a trust that allowed us to confront problems, an accountability that helped us overcome sin and a bond that has held us together through thick and thin.

For over ten years we have maintained a closeness in spite of personal disagreements and misunderstandings, location changes (Kathy is now 2,000 miles away instead of two blocks) and busier schedules.

Now men, you may be thinking (as my husband just informed me), *That's all fine and good for women, but men just aren't that way. We really don't want to share our feelings that much or feel the need to exchange warm fuzzies. Just give us a good Sean*

> Enrich someone's life today with a warm word of encouragement. Both of you will be better for it.

Connery action-adventure with a wide-screen television or a workshop where we can use power tools, and we can bond just fine.

Apparently Sociologist Janet Lever agrees that there is a notable difference in the way we interact, and it begins at an early age. Lever reports:

> There is usually an open show of affection between little girls, both physically in the form of hand-holding and orally through "love-notes" that reaffirm how special each is to the other. Although boys are likely to have best friends as well, their friendships tend to be less intimate and expressive than girls. Those affections are virtually unknown among boys, and the confidences that boys share are more likely to be "group secrets" than expressions of private thoughts and feelings.[1]

It's a no-brainer that men like to center their time together around activity rather than confiding their deepest secrets. It would be simplistic of me to suggest that they do otherwise, to force themselves to be comfortable with "sharing." But what I fear is that by staying completely in their comfort zone, they will isolate themselves from each other and adopt a lone ranger mentality. Alan Loy McGinnis, author of the best-selling *The Friendship Factor,* says that America's leading psychologists and therapists estimate that only ten percent of all men ever have any real friends.[2] The decade-long research on 5,000 men and women by Michael McGill, published in 1985, corroborates this. He reports:

> To say that men have no intimate friends seems on the surface too harsh . . . but it is not far from the truth. Even the most intimate of friendships rarely approach the depth of disclosure a woman commonly has with many other women.[3]

But is that the way it should be? Don't men need each other as much as women need to relate to other women? Christ thought so. His ministry was centered in deep friendships with the Twelve, whom He repeatedly called "friends" (John 15:13-15), and there was also the inner circle of three with whom He formed an even deeper friendship and to whom He bared His heart.[4]

There are more biblical examples of male friendships such as:

- Jesus sending the disciples out in twos (Mark 6:7)
- Paul traveling with Barnabas (Acts 15)
- Barnabas and Mark (Acts 15)
- Paul and Timothy (1 Timothy 1)
- David and Jonathan (1 Samuel 20)

Though friendship has fallen on hard times these days, especially among men, it doesn't have to stay that way. Once we admit our inherent need for friendships and that it is indeed biblical and Christlike to pursue and nurture them, we can't help but be compelled to do something about it.

Not that we don't have friends. Most of us have countless people we enjoy spending time with and are involved with on a regular basis. But what is becoming rare is the kind of friends that are involved in our lives: long-lasting and constant.

- Do we have friends that really know us, our past experiences and our future dreams?
- Do we know more about them than just what they do for a living, how many kids they have, where they live?
- Are we the kind of friends who are faithful to show up when there is a need?

Two months ago, my husband Mike and I were getting ready to move into a home where we were the general contractors. We had done a lot of the work ourselves and by the end we were dog tired. That's when Mike's friend Steve just started showing up to help. He painted walls, helped with the wood flooring, finished electrical

Friendship: Heart to Heart

sockets—whatever we were working on is where he enthusiastically jumped in. His joy was contagious. It helped get us through those last few days when we wanted to give up.

Steve knew our need and made a choice to invest himself not just for our home, but for our hearts. His faithfulness, and that of the many others who brought us meals and helped us finish on time, pulled us through an emotionally difficult time. That's because when we invest in others, and they in us, we can't help but be more fulfilled. More relaxed. More confident. More energized to tackle whatever life brings our way.

Now the $60,000 question: how do we get there? While many characteristics contribute to the health of each friendship, there are some that have a more powerful and lasting effect than others. During my almost forty years of developing friendships and observing the making and breaking of them, both in my own life and vicariously, four key components have consistently surfaced. The presence of these four characteristics is a strong indicator of the depth and durability of a friendship. Likewise, the lack of them seems to be a fairly valid indicator of that friendship's certain demise.

The key word to remember in understanding these four points is the word GIFT. And since this rare kind of friendship is exactly that—a gift—doesn't it warrant some effort on our part to nurture and care for it? Isn't it worth just a little bit of extra time and mental energy?

> He has the right to criticize who has the heart to help.
>
> *Abraham Lincoln*

To develop and build friendships, we need to:

G ive encouragement
I nvest time
F orgive completely
T alk less; listen more

Every enduring friendship will exhibit these four traits. And while they may vary in degree and consistency with each friend, they will be an integral part of the committed devotion that yields true and strong friendships.

As you know, nothing good comes without a price. It will be work, to be sure. If it were easy, we'd all have a lot of close friends and we would keep the same ones year after year. Unfortunately that is the rare exception rather than the rule. It seems the tendency is to keep a friend until there is a misunderstanding, disappointment or controversy.

Then, rather than confronting the issues at hand with gentleness and tact, moving toward a mature resolution, we simply drift apart. Sometimes that can take a year or so, sometimes only a few short weeks. "Out with the old, in with the new" becomes our adage, and we never taste the sweet fruit that comes from nurturing and growing a healthy and enduring friendship.

To love and be loved, to understand and be understood, to encourage and be encouraged by a friend you respect and value is certainly worth the investment. And when we learn how to nur-

> A deep, enduring friendship brings oxygen to our soul.

ture that relationship with the four keys: encouragement, time, forgiveness and intentional listening, we invest in a rare treasure indeed—a friendship anchored by self-sacrificing virtues.

What better way to begin to cultivate a deeper friendship than to learn about the resplendent joy of encouragement.

Key #1: Give Encouragement

It started as such an enjoyable conversation, just pleasant chatter between two close friends about "spiritual" issues. Suzi and I were on the leadership team for the women's ministry at our church and we were brainstorming about new material we wanted to teach. We were enthusiastically sharing our ideas and even through the phone we could sense the mutual excitement and anticipation.

There was only one glitch. Toward the end of the conversation Suzi said, "Oh, by the way, I've lined up some people to host a prayer breakfast in a few weeks. I hope that's OK."

Now, in my mind I thought, *Fantastic! That is such a great idea!* But what came out of my mouth was anything but encouraging. In fact, it was downright critical.

"Don't you think you and I should have discussed this before you asked them? Are we a team or not? Did you think to confirm the date on the church calendar? More than likely we'll face a conflict there."

Conflict, indeed. I had just created one and didn't even have the good sense to recognize it. That is, until Suzi said with a rather tight and curt voice, "Laurie, you are being offensive!"

Silence.

At first I thought she was kidding. We'd been close friends for over two years and never had words before. "I'm sorry," I said, "is something wrong?" Well, duh.

Silence again.

> Kindness is the golden chain by which society is bound together.
>
> *Goethe*

Finally, she said in a soft and cracking voice (the kind you have when a dear friend has just verbally punched you in the stomach), "I need to go." The next thing I heard was "click."

Whoa—what happened there?, I asked myself, still pitifully in denial. Self-protection is such a powerful defense mechanism, but rarely is it truthful.

Fortunately, I knew someone who would tell me the whole truth and nothing but the truth, so help him God—my husband Mike. He had been on the receiving end of some of my undiscerning comments and not only survived them, but somehow still cherished me and accepted me—warts and all.

After I stated my version of the conversation, swaying it ever so slightly in my favor, he looked me straight in the eye and said, "Laurie, far too often your words are biting and critical. Then you wonder why people get upset. My dear, you need to find a way to speak love and encouragement to your friends and family as consistently as you do to your audiences."

Ouch!

His honesty stung, but I knew he was right. I began to digest his advice, and after swallowing a big slice of humble pie, I allowed myself to appreciate the valuable truth in his words. I had not been encouraging to Suzi. I hadn't offered her one crumb of appreciation, let alone a feast of praise that would have lifted her spirits and spurred her on.

Now I was the miserable one. My spirit became heavy with regret and I began to fear that I had permanently damaged our precious friendship. Proverbs 18:21 says, "The tongue has the power of life and death." I was beginning to realize that what I had done was no small thing. I remembered my stinging words and felt ashamed that they had passed through my unguarded lips. Unfortunately, words are a lot like toothpaste. Once they are out, you can never put them back in. And they often leave a mess.

I called Suzi to apologize, but she wouldn't answer her phone. I cried into my pillow most of the night.

Florence Littauer is one of the most gifted teachers, speakers and authors of our time. In her best-selling book, *Silver Boxes: The Gift of Encouraging Words,* she advises us that every time we speak, our words should be so uplifting to the person listening that they feel they are receiving a beautiful gift, wrapped in a silver box.[5]

I hardly think Suzi would have considered my words a gift.

I wonder, friend, have you taken the time to give away any silver boxes lately? Men, have you reached out to encourage a friend you know is struggling? Women, who needs a word of praise from you?

Perhaps you haven't offended anyone with your words in the last few days, but I wonder how many of your "friends" doubt their importance to you because you have simply done nothing. Isn't it possible that omission is its own form of discouragement?

Consequences of discouragement

There is always a price to be paid for discouraging someone. You wound the other person's heart and you fill your own with regret. Nothing positive comes from it, only more pain. Sometimes the price is as high as the death of a friendship.

Think about the last time you felt discouraged by someone's words or neglected from the lack of them. Did it endear you to them or drive a wedge between you? Naturally, the walls go up. If the infraction is serious enough, you spend less time together. There is less depth to your conversations. The relationship becomes surface-oriented. The intimacy is lost. The friend once valued as a close confidante becomes a distant acquaintance.

Another consequence is that discouragement attacks self-esteem. It reaches down to the very core of what a person believes about himself. It sends a profound message: you are inadequate and unimportant. And for whatever reason, it sounds believable. Some people rise above it; some internalize it as truth and are incapacitated by it for the rest of their lives.

I've been on the receiving end of discouragement, so I know firsthand how devastating it can be. In grade school, I was often teased by classmates for giving the wrong answer. "What a dummy." "Wrong again." "Lights are on, nobody's home," they would laugh.

But what I remember most were the times when some of my friends joined in. While I laughed along with them, pretending it didn't bother me, their words pierced me like a double-edged sword. After all, if a friend said it, it must be true. Their discouraging words became part of the script I played in my head that told me who I was—a dummy. By the time I was in high school I had given up on studying and probably would have been voted most likely to fail had there been such a category.

Yes, words do have the power of life and death, and discouragement from careless words or neglect is the fastest way to crush a person's spirit and kill a friendship.

Friendship: Heart to Heart

The fruit of encouragement

Encouragement, on the other hand, is inspiring and character-building. Don't you find yourself drawn to people who speak kindness to you, who give you verbal gifts of affirmation and esteem? We love to be around people who lift us up. It is a natural response to encouragement, just as pulling away or building a wall is our natural response to discouragement.

Encouragement always has a positive effect. If this weren't true, people wouldn't be so hungry for it. When I speak on encouragement, I often have the audience use a 3 x 5 card to write what they appreciate about the person sitting next to them. Usually the participants know each other and have no problem with this exercise. When they exchange cards, they are often shocked at the good others see in them. It is like a shot in the arm to the entire group. Afterward they thank each other, laughing and smiling.

People sometimes tell me that this exercise was the highlight of their week! I have received letters from folks who tell me they still have their cards—three years later! I have a special place where I keep cards of encouragement that friends have sent me, and every now and then I pull a few out and reread them. It's like a pat on the back to have someone appreciate and believe in you. And it is a good reminder to me not to be lazy or procrastinate with encouraging words for others.

> When I want to speak, let me think first. Is it true? Is it kind? Is it necessary? If not, let it be left unsaid.
>
> *Maltbie D. Babcock*

I was speaking at a conference two years ago and my good friend, Nancy, was in the audience. Afterward, while I was counseling some of the ladies in my seminar, she left a note on my podium. It was written on one of her bank deposit slips. (Is she trusting or what?) All it said was, "Laurie, I am so proud of you. Love, Nancy." It was such a poignant moment for me, especially considering the profound discouragement I had heard as a child. Her words communicated support, respect and honor. I felt hugged all day because Nancy took the time to communicate encouragement to me. I still have the note.

Encouragement is a free and yet priceless gift, for how could we ever put a price on the joy, cheer and assurance it brings? It is impossible to qualify its goodness but it feeds the heart like Miracle Grow feeds my plants. The exponential growth is amazing.

Give it a try

Note-writing is a simple way to begin to communicate encouragement. While women seem to communicate their feelings more easily to one another (as Nancy did to me), men find it easier to communicate appreciation for accomplishment. I can't imagine one of Mike's friends leaving a note on his desk, written on a bank slip, intimating words of affirmation. Not that they aren't wonderful, thoughtful men. It's just not one of those guy things we discussed earlier. Men seem to be much more comfortable jotting a note on their professional stationary (our pastor does this quite often) or sending a quick e-mail, thanking someone for their help during a project.

Use whatever method works for you and follow through. The influence of your kind words will be powerful indeed! Why keep your appreciation for someone a secret in your own heart? Let it be known and watch it grow.

I love the Harriet Beecher Stowe quote that says, "If you think a compliment is due someone, now is the time to give it, because a tombstone cannot hear." What are you waiting for? Don't miss the opportunity to lift someone's spirits. You'll lift yours in the process and your friendship will take a giant leap forward.

Initially it can be easier to write encouragement to someone rather than speak it because it gives you more time to think it through. An added benefit is that it also gives the receiver a tangible piece of paper to help him or her remember what you said or reread when feeling down. It's difficult to understand the immeasurable influence of our words, but once we grasp the breadth of it we'll realize that every conversation has the power to lift or demean, inspire or deflate, gouge or soothe. With every sentence we can communicate love and acceptance or rejection and discouragement. Either way, the words of encouragement you speak or the words you write will leave an indelible mark of love on your friends *and* on your friendship.

Simple ways to show it

There are many ways we can communicate encouragement. It just takes a little thoughtfulness to make it specific to each friend, a little confidence to know that it will be well received and a little ambition to follow through. If it's important enough, you'll make sure it happens. You know it—and so do your friends.

Here are some suggestions to help get you started:

- Send a card to tell someone what you appreciate about her personality or character, as well as for tasks she does or projects she completes. It's always a boost to have your actions appreciated, but how much more for who you are!
- A phone call to see how her week is going lets her know that you have been thinking about her, and that communicates a caring attitude. Make an effort to know what projects she is involved in and how her family is doing.

> If I can stop one heart from breaking, I shall not live in vain.
>
> *Emily Dickinson*

- Don't miss an opportunity to compliment someone verbally. A kind and genuine compliment doesn't puff up, it builds up and helps your friend reach for her potential.
- Smile, give a hearty handshake, an enthusiastic hug, a pat on the back, even a high five. These are all instant ways to communicate that you are glad to see your friends. They'll remember your enthusiasm.
- Treat a friend to lunch. Time slips away all too quickly and before you know it, a week turns into a month, a month into a year and so on. Lunch is a convenient time to catch up on each others' lives while protecting your evenings for family time. (Keep it same-sex friends if you or the other person is married. Why open the door to temptation?)
- Thoughtful gifts are always appreciated, but they needn't be expensive to be of value. Does your friend collect anything? Does he have a favorite sports team or compete in a sports activity? Use your imagination. He'll be encouraged by your generosity and how well you know him.
- Volunteer to work on a project with him. (Here you go, guys!)

- Add his name to your prayer list and pray for him on the same day each week.
- Include him in a get-together.

Remember, even the smallest act or word of encouragement will go a long way. Who can you give yours to?

Key #2: Invest Time

Just as giving encouragement helps build a stronger friendship, investing time is another significant way to strengthen the ties that bind. I always looked forward to my weekly tennis match with my friend Diane. We were perfect opponents for each other because we had equal ability, and although we played our hearts out, we really didn't care who won. It was invigorating and refreshing even though after an hour or so we had to drag our exhausted bodies off the court.

I remember those days with fondness because of the intense exercise and camaraderie they provided. But, in hindsight, what rejuvenated me the most were the conversations we had afterward, leaning against the side of our cars drinking water and sharing the events of the week. We would laugh about recipe blunders and laundry mistakes; share bewilderment over the challenges of raising babies, toddlers and adolescents at the same time; bemoan the tax hike on families; and share our dreams of what we would do when our children left the nest and we no longer had the responsibility of molding their lives. Our hearts were entwined because we invested time in our friendship. And that is what I miss.

Four years ago, Diane moved to the country. Although we vowed to stay in touch and occasionally still run into each other, the friendship has all but died. Lunch appointments were broken, calls unreturned. It's not that anything nasty was ever said. We didn't have a falling out or a misunderstanding. We simply stopped spending time together because it was no longer convenient.

Proximity proved to be a daunting foe, and when you don't stay connected, the relationship stops growing. You fall out of touch with each other's needs and joys and dreams. You trade intimacy for courtesy.

When Diane stopped attending our church some time ago, I called to see if there was a problem I could help with since it was very unlike her to miss a service. She assured me that everything was fine but that her children's schedules had taken over her life. She hoped I still knew how much she appreciated my friendship. When I hesitated, she added that she still considered me one of her closest friends and even if five years went by without us seeing each other, we would always be the best of friends.

I'm afraid that seems unrealistic to me. How can we possibly be the best of friends when she doesn't know what is going on in my life, nor I hers? She doesn't know that Evan broke his arm— twice—or that he took up diving last summer. She doesn't know that Allie is now baby-sitting and playing on her first basketball team. She doesn't know that David will turn twenty next month and that I'm feeling more than a little anxiety about his being on his own. She doesn't know how much I missed my dad this year on the anniversary of his death, or how much I felt her absence at my surprise birthday party. I shudder to think what I have missed in her life. A close friendship cannot survive unless there is regular time invested. It's as simple as that.

Long distance

Time investment can come in all different forms. Even though my friends Kathy and Julie live out of state, we have kept our friendships alive by following this principle: We e-mail regularly, call often, write occasionally and visit as funds and schedules allow. We remember each other's birthdays and other important dates. We've made a choice to work at our friendships and to view the commitment as an investment to which both parties must contribute.

Hospitality

Three years ago, after hearing David Roadcup speak on hospitality, Mike and I felt convicted. We wanted to be good stewards of the home that God had given us and we wanted to build closer relationships with our friends. Realizing that friendships must be nurtured by investing time (the one commodity that we have the least of), we made a pledge to use Sunday evening dinner to invite friends over as a way to continue relationships already established, and also get to know new friends.

Since then, we have had over 300 people in our home for everything from tacos to turkey. It has been an incredible blessing to us and a small price to pay to share laughter and love with friends we now know better. The investment of time has given us back a priceless gift indeed.

Key #3: Forgive Completely

Giving encouragement and investing time are super-effective ways to build a strong foundation for friendship. However, if forgiveness is not extended during difficult times, the rela-

> He who plants thorns must never expect to gather roses.
>
> *Anonymous*

tionship will crumble and we will have built the foundation in vain.

I awoke with swollen eyes and a new resolve to humbly ask forgiveness from Suzi. Even though it was barely 7 a.m., I said a quick prayer and dialed her number. She answered.

"Suzi, I am so sorry! Please, will you forgive me?" I blurted out, unable to suppress the sobs. "I know I was totally insensitive and critical, and I am so sorry I hurt you."

"Laurie, I was so angry when I hung up last night I just couldn't talk. I couldn't believe you were saying those things to me and I didn't want to say anything back in the heat of the moment. Yes, I forgive you. Of course I forgive you. I was hoping we could talk today because I wanted to apologize for getting so angry and hanging up. That was uncalled for. Would you forgive me for that?"

I felt almost guilty granting her request since I was entirely responsible for the incident. "It's already forgotten," I assured her.

Tears brought relief for us both and at the end of our conversation we were even able to laugh about the foolishness of it all. A few days later when we met for lunch, we hugged and knew the slate was clean. A relational disaster had been averted for one reason, and one reason only: forgiveness. Complete forgiveness. No grudges held. No seed of bitterness allowed to take root, only to later rear its ugly head. No ammunition held for the future. Our friendship was made stronger, but it could have so easily gone the other way if there had not been the willingness to forgive and forget.

Often, even if we think we've forgiven a friend's offense, we have the tendency to quietly hold on to it. We're not angry on the surface but deep down we still feel resentment. We've swept it under the rug for the time being and managed to put a smile on our face, but inside we're still stewing on it. It's only a matter of time before the relationship is destroyed from all that pent-up anger. While I'm not implying some deep hurts can ever be totally erased from the memory, I am suggesting that when it does come to mind we don't dwell on it for one second! We must learn to take our thoughts captive to make them obedient to Christ (2 Corinthians 10:5) or they will keep us captive to anger.

When we say, "I can forgive, but I cannot forget," it's really just another way of saying, "I will not forgive." Henry Ward Beecher said, "Forgiveness ought to be like a canceled note—torn in two, and burned up, so it can never be shown again."

How many times have we forgiven someone, then later said to them during a misunderstanding, "This is just like last time. Remember when you _____. You always do _____. You never do _____." How do we know they always or never do anything unless we are still holding on to the previous offense?

We must let it go! To forgive and forget gives health to the person doing the forgiving, but holding on to a friend's transgressions keeps us from two things:

1. Building a deeper friendship with him or her;
2. Having a peaceful heart which brings health to our whole body.

Imagine you have a room in your home filled with old, broken furniture. But it wasn't always that way. It used to be so inviting. The chairs were overstuffed and cozy, and each had its own matching ottoman to rest your feet on. They were perfect for reading the paper or for falling asleep halfway through the news. The end table that sat nuzzled between the two chairs was a solid cherry, handcrafted antique, with nary a scratch on it. There you liked to set your Bible because your moments in that room were peaceful and memorable, inviting meaningful reflection and meditation.

> Many a friendship, long, loyal, and self-sacrificing, rested at first on no thicker a foundation than a kind word.
>
> *Frederick W. Faber*

But all that changed when your friend Katie visited with her twin toddlers and ninety-pound Labrador. While playing hide-and-seek in your special room, Katie thoughtlessly allowed the twins to jump on the chairs, poking large holes through the plush cushions and beautiful fabric. There was chaos everywhere when the dog's leash got wrapped around the beautiful cherry table and he began chewing on it to break free, leaving irreparable gouging and splintering.

And then, as quickly as they had arrived and ruined your furniture, they were gone in a whirlwind with apologies offered and a polite forgiveness extended from you. Since then Katie has stopped by many times and offered to replace the furniture but you won't hear of it. Instead, you assure her, "It's fine. Really." But when you walk by that room, you are constantly reminded of her offense, and you just want to scream. Months go by and the room goes unused. You wish so badly you could enjoy your special room again but you won't let go of what is broken to make room for the beauty of new.

When we allow our hearts to be filled with resentment over what could've been forgiven and thrown into the sea of forgetfulness, what space is left for restoration? It's as if a part of our hearts becomes unusable and we have no room for the beauty of reconciliation. There is less room to be trusting, less room to be content and joyful.

Forgiving and forgetting cleanses our hearts and gets rid of the ugly brokenness, leaving room for meaningful friendships that exclude beauty and strength.

Take a look inside

Sometimes the only way to get past an offense or hurt from a friend is to discuss it openly together. It makes me tighten up just thinking about it, because confrontation is risky. It's painful and has ended many a friendship. But occasionally there are issues along the way that must be addressed and understood before you can move on.

If you have a friend who values your relationship enough to risk being vulnerable and tells you that your words have been hurtful, your friendship has the potential to recover and even mature to a deeper level. But only on one condition: that you humble yourself enough to be introspective about your weaknesses and your ability to make mistakes.

I'll never forget several years ago (before the Suzi incident) when my dear friend Rene called me one morning and asked if we could have lunch. There was something important that she wanted to discuss with me and I could tell by the tone of her voice that it was not about the new spring fashions. I agreed to meet with her and when I arrived at the restaurant, she was already there waiting. After giving the waiter our order, she took a deep breath and said that she hoped I would take the conversation in the light in which she intended.

All of a sudden, I wasn't so hungry. She calmly and quietly recounted to me a recent conversation I had had with another friend—about her. I had criticized her and obviously thought she wouldn't find out. Now here she was confronting me with the awful truth, and to make matters even more embarrassing, delivering it with gentleness and maturity. Talk about feeling like a jerk. My stomach had been churning since I sat down, but I knew I had to take a big bite of humble pie, indigestion or not, and humbly apologize for my mistake.

That was over ten years ago and Rene and I are still close friends. I'm so thankful for her courage to confront me and forgive me. And I'm thankful that pride didn't get the best of me (as it so often does) and I was able to apologize immediately.

That incident actually strengthened our relationship and helped me learn to be a better friend. It made me establish a rule for myself that day that I would never speak a word about someone unless I could comfortably say it to his or her face. But the greater lesson was about the awesome power of gentle confrontation and forgiveness, and it so powerfully demonstrated how it can strengthen the ties of a friendship when it is done with love and respect.

When Rene gave me permission to use her story, I asked her how she had prepared for our "lunch" discussion. There were three rules she made for herself:

1. She prayed about it and asked, "How likely is it that this confrontation will change Laurie's behavior?" (Fortunately, she had some confidence that my heart would be open to it.) Our motive for confrontation should be changed behavior rather than the release of our anger. If the person is unlikely to change, why do it?
2. Second, she made sure she was over her anger before she spoke with me so she could communicate calmly and respectfully. She asked God to remove it from her heart and meditated on James 1:20: "Man's anger does not bring about the righteous life that God desires." When your anger is healed (for Rene that was two days), ask the Lord to give you the right words and the courage needed to deliver them. Then stick to the behavior and don't assassinate the person's character.
3. Thirdly, she made up her mind that she wouldn't bring it up again, nor did she ever discuss it with any of our other friends.

Is that integrity or what? Her godliness was a great example to me of how to extend grace. No wonder people admire her.

The kiss of death

Equally, the unwillingness to forgive can mean the death of a friendship. It may happen right after a huge verbal blowup, or it may be as subtle as one misunderstood word that begins an emotional drift. But be sure of this: absence of forgiveness means separation. It may even damage other friendships and relationships, because hurting people hurt people.

Corrie Ten Boom, a Nazi camp survivor, said, "Forgiveness is not an emotion. It is an act of the will, and the will can function regardless of the temperature of the heart." What a powerful statement from a woman who had every reason to withhold forgiveness. She had watched her sister Betsy die a slow and agonizing death from the cruelties of the Nazi officers. After the war ended, she was confronted by a man she vividly remembered as one of their guards. He was in the audience as she spoke on the great love of God and how anyone could find forgiveness for his sins. The following is an excerpt from her book, *Clippings from My Notebook*.

> After my talk, he approached me and thrust his hand out to meet mine. "A fine message, Fraulein! How good it is to know that, as you

> Blessed are they who are pleasant to live with.
>
> *Anonymous*

say, all our sins are at the bottom of the sea!" And I, who had just spoken of forgiveness, fumbled in my pocketbook rather than take that hand. "Since the war, I have become a Christian. I know that God forgives me for the cruel things I did there, but I would like to hear it from your lips as well. Fraulein—" again the hand came out—"will you forgive me?"

It could not have been many seconds that he stood there, hand held out, but to me it seemed hours as I wrestled with the most difficult thing I had ever had to do. Since the end of the war I had established a home in Holland for victims of Nazi brutality. Those who were able to forgive their former enemies were able to successfully return to the outside world and rebuild their lives, no matter what the physical and emotional scars. Those who nursed bitterness remained invalids. It was as simple and as horrible as that. And still I stood there with the coldness clutching my heart. "Jesus, help me!" I prayed silently.

And so woodenly, mechanically, I thrust my hand into the one stretched out to me. And as I did, an incredible thing took place. The current started in my shoulder, raced down my arm, sprang into our joined hands. And then this healing warmth seemed to flood my whole being, bringing tears to my eyes.

"I forgive you, brother!" I cried. "With all my heart!"

For a long time we grasped each other's hands, the former guard and the former prisoner. I had never known God's love and forgiveness as intensely as I did then. [6]

Corrie forgave to the depth that most of us will never have to. She chose to extend forgiveness to an enemy because she knew she would receive freedom for her own heart. How much more should we be willing to forgive our friends? Only then will we know peace in our hearts. And only where there is peace can there be warmth and healing.

Martin Luther King Jr. said, "Forgiveness should not be just an occasional act, but a permanent attitude."

Go on. Make that phone call, write that letter, send that e-mail to that friend you haven't spoken with for a while. Let go of the pride that keeps you prisoner. Stretch out your hand to ask forgiveness and to give it. Don't worry about how you'll sound. It's so much more ridiculous to nurse a grudge than to risk the unknown. Perhaps you too will feel a flood of healing warmth come into your heart with an intensity you have never known.

Key #4: Talk less; listen more

I was only twenty-one and it was the fanciest dinner party I'd ever been to. The kind that would make Martha Stewart wish she'd been a guest. Beautiful ice sculptures, decadent food I couldn't pronounce, busy waiters in tails and white gloves carefully pandering to each guest. Soft jazz music playing in the background.

My upper-management executive friend Julie had invited me to her annual Christmas gala, held at the most expensive hotel in town. For dinner, I was strategically surrounded by unfamiliar faces, no doubt a ploy by Julie to stimulate conversation amongst those of us less well known.

Luckily I was seated across from a gentleman who was an engaging and interesting conversationalist. He asked thought-provoking questions and seemed genuinely absorbed in my every reply. So much so that I felt encouraged to tell story upon story of what I had experienced in life as he listened with undivided attention. The night flew by and I felt relieved that I had handled my first big shindig with grace and ease.

Upon exiting the hotel, reality hit when I heard him tell one of his friends that he had gotten stuck across from a real Chatty Cathy and was relieved the night was over.

Chatty Cathy! How could he say that when he had hung on my every word? He seemed so engrossed in what I had to say and kept asking such intriguing questions. We had connected, hadn't we? We knew so much about each other, or at least he did about me. . . .

The best lessons are sometimes the hardest. I learned that night about the true art of conversation—asking intentional, unselfish questions, affirming each statement with an appropriate response, unwavering eye contact, and above all else, listen much more than you talk. Believe me, that is a lesson I don't ever intend to forget.

Listening is an integral part of every relationship, but especially so in friendship. Skilled conversing shows that you care and helps the person speaking to feel important. Often our friends don't need our advice as much as they need us to really listen.

It was one of those harried days for me. I had too much to do and not enough hours to get it all done in. I was running out of the school after an event for Evan, my second-grader, and ran into my friend, Nancy. As we quickly passed, she said, "Laurie, please pray for me today. Life is falling apart."

Whoa. I came to a dead stop as she hurried by. "Nancy, wait," I said as I caught her arm. "What's going on? Do you want to talk about it? Why don't we go in the activity room and chat?" For the next hour and a half, Nancy confided in me about the bitter argument she had just had with a family member and how there didn't seem to be any chance or desire for resolution.

What we love we shall grow to resemble.

St. Bernard

She was being sued by her neighbor for taking down her fence, of all things. She had no time for herself, let alone her husband.

On top of that, she was struggling with how to care for her aging parents who lived three hours away. Nancy's anger and tension were obvious as she began to explain her problems in detail. I listened intently, nodded my head occasionally and asked appropriate questions, letting her know what she was saying was important. At the end of our conversation, we prayed for wisdom and guidance over each issue, and I hugged her and reminded her I loved her.

Even though I didn't fix any of her problems, I helped her release her anxiety and anger by praying and by simply listening. She felt calmer and more at peace as she left the school, in spite of the fact that the upsetting situations had not changed. All I gave her was what she had given me so many times—a listening ear and a moment of understanding and sympathy.

I'm struck at the number of times I have utilized my new listening skills with friends, having never offered one piece of advice, only to hear them say, "Hey, thanks for letting me vent. I feel so much better. You've really helped me."

I did? Oh yeah, it's the listening that counts. When you listen to people, you tell them they are important. When you monopolize the conversation, you say you are important. We all know people who greet us enthusiastically and then barely give us a chance to say we're fine before they unload their newest crisis. If you're developing good conversation skills, you will inevitably encounter this because people are so hungry for significance. Chances are, folks who monopolize don't have any lasting friendships because they drain the life right out of them, just like I did to the gentleman at the dinner party.

Even if you are under a mountain of stress (who isn't?) and suffering through a personal crisis, don't always center the conversation around you. You be the one to ask the heart-to-heart questions that make your friend feel cared for and important.

Here's the true litmus test: do you know as much (or more) about your friends than they know about you?

Sure, there will be times when you need to share more than you listen because of the nature of the situation. Just make sure you balance it often with unselfish questions, anchoring it with genuine concern. Otherwise, the friendship will become lopsided and sink faster than the *Titanic*. Life is enough of a drain. Be a friend that listens well and often.

Conclusion

We should seize every opportunity to Give encouragement, Invest time, Forgive completely and Talk less, if we are to know the sweet fruit of intimate friendship. It may sometimes force us out of our comfort zone, but it is God's will for us to love Him and His people. Remembering to treat our friends like a GIFT will keep us connected heart to heart and make us healthier for a lifetime.

Discussion Questions

1. Think back to a time when your heart was lightened by an encouraging word. Who was it from and how did it make you feel? How do you encourage others? Who is someone you can lift up this week?
2. How can we apply Proverbs 27:17—"As iron sharpens iron, so one man sharpens another"—to encourage each other?
3. Read Proverbs 20:3 and 25:15. What can this teach us about confrontation? What is your style of resolving conflict? Is there someone right now you need to forgive?

4. Read Hebrews 10:24-25. What was the purpose of "meeting together"? How do you like to "invest time" in friendships? What is one step you can take to reach out to a friend and spend time with him or her?
5. Read First Samuel 23:15-18. What were three things Jonathan did to help David through a crisis? Since it is God's will for you to nurture your friendships, how can you follow Jonathan's example?

Endnotes

1. Janet Leever, "Sex Differences in the Games Children Play," *Social Problems*, 23 (1976), pp. 478-487.

2. Alan Loy McGinnis, *The Friendship Factor* (Minneapolis: Augsburg, 1979), p. 11.

3. Harold B. Smith, "Best Friend," *Marriage Partnership*, Summer 1988, p. 126.

4. R. Kent Hughes, *The Disciplines of a Godly Man* (Wheaton: Crossway Books, 1991), p. 60.

5. Florence Littauer, *Silver Boxes: The Gift of Encouraging Words* (Dallas: Word, 1989), p. 6.

6. Reprinted by permission of Thomas Nelson Publishers from the book entitled *Clippings from My Notebook*, copyright date 1982 by Corrie Ten Boom.

Chapter 2

Marriage: One Heart

I always cry at weddings. It happens so consistently that I've learned just to expect it and plan for it. Mike keeps an extra hankie in his pocket and I carry extra make-up. I'm not sure what chokes me up more: the meaningful ceremony, the sentimental music, the beautiful processional, the eloquent vows—or the fact that this couple, now enjoying one of the most important moments of their lives, has only a fifty-fifty chance of making it last. It's heartbreaking to think that such a beautiful and passionate beginning could so quickly produce such intense pain.

Unfortunately it is a scenario I know all too well. My first marriage lasted only four years and ended with our young son caught in the bitter crossfire. I find it difficult to pen the words that describe the emotional devastation and trauma a family is forced to face when promises are broken and lives are crushed. Suffice it to say that a very significant part of me died and I wondered if I would ever be whole again.

> There is no more lovely, friendly, charming a relationship, communion or company than a good marriage.
>
> Martin Luther

Yes, I cry for both reasons. Yet, just as the breaking up of a marriage is profoundly horrible, the enduring love that can keep it together is immeasurably glorious.

This year I'm celebrating fifteen years of marriage to Mike, whom I love and adore even more than the day we spoke our vows. There isn't a day that goes by that I don't look at him and think, *Man, am I blessed!* I'm always pleasantly surprised and thrilled that he still feels the same about me. It's not that we have a marriage made in heaven, because, frankly, there isn't one. The idea was created in heaven and the institution of marriage was all part of the grand scheme, but every relationship is forged out between us and our partners here on earth. God may be the Master Designer, but we are the contractors. It is up to us to daily oversee the maintenance of it.

Stephen T. Wyatt, author of *Behind the Tent Flaps*, says:

> The scene is bad, people. Real bad. But I wonder if it wouldn't help, even just a little bit, to realize that it's never been perfect? At least not since the day Adam and Eve got booted from the Garden. Ever since that fateful day, marriage has been anything but a tiptoe through the tulips.[1]

Another wit has described marriage as a three-ring circus: First you have the engagement ring, then comes the wedding ring and finally you get the suffering!

While mildly amusing, too often it feels like the truth. Couples are exiting marriage at breakneck speed. What makes it so hard is that building a healthy, vital relationship requires full and complete denial of one's self to create oneness with a partner who is fully and completely imperfect. At first glance that proposition sounds lopsided. I mean, why be in a marriage if all I'm going to do is give, give, give? How fair is that?

According to Dawn Bradley Berry, marriage expert and author of *Divorce Recovery*, as many as half of all marriage partners have decided, "No, it's not fair. I deserve more than this and I'm not going to put up with your selfishness anymore. See ya."[2]

And if divorce is not their primary means of soothing their pain, there is a good chance unfaithfulness will be. According to Willard F. Harley Jr., author of *His Needs, Her Needs*, his twenty-five years of marriage counseling led him to believe that of the partners who do stay married, half will go through the agony of an affair.[3] That leaves only twenty-five percent who are enjoying marriage! Heaven help us.

Yes, I would agree with Mr. Wyatt. The scene is bad. Real bad. But not hopeless.

While acknowledging these grim statistics and knowing personally how devastating the deterioration of marriage is, when I married Mike fifteen years ago, I still believed that our marriage could be different, that somehow we could mesh our two lives together and create one heart. I wanted a marriage that was not ego-centered but faith-centered, honoring God so that even our conversations and thoughts of each other would be a sweet aroma to Him. Against the odds, I wanted us to have the kind of marriage that only twenty-five percent of couples do!

So for all these years I have consumed copious amounts of books and articles, listened to tapes and attended seminars that give instruction on everything from how to choose a spouse to how to please him (or her) on your fiftieth anniversary! (Many of those resources are included in the recommended reading at the end of this book.)

After fifteen years of (mostly) blissful marriage, it feels good to report that Mike and I are beating the odds. Our marriage has never been better and apparently it shows. We are often asked by other couples what our "secret" is, and we can honestly say there is only one: We live by God's rules, not our own.

Yes, it's that simple. God-centered, not ego-centered. We both die to ourselves every day so that we work for the common good of "us" instead of "me." It's a choice. Black and white.

What's not so simple is what we do in those moments when we don't *want* to die to ourselves. Sure, it's easy for me to be unselfish when Mike is helping around the house, getting home from work on time, praising me for being such an involved mom—appreciating me. But when he's tired, crabby and demanding (in other words, human), there is a clashing of needs and egos that is anything but a sweet aroma.

What we've learned from the Bible is that God has certain guidelines that help us get along with our spouses. When we live by them, we thrive. When we don't, it's ugly. Now when people ask us about our secret, we identify three specific rules that bring us back together:

- Submission
- Respectful communication
- Passion

We've also learned that while no marriage is made in heaven, a healthy marriage can give you a taste of it. And it is unforgettably delicious.

How about you? Got a sweet tooth?

Submission Is Not a 4-Letter Word

Submission. Just the word alone makes us bristle, doesn't it?

My synonym finder used phrases like "throw in the towel," "give up the ship" and "grin and bear it" to define "submit." No wonder we run for cover.

I was caught on video during our marriage vows, raising my eyebrow when the minister said submission should be part of our promise to each other. Raising one eyebrow is not the same as raising two, which indicates surprise. When I raise one eyebrow, it means, "What planet are you from?"

And there it is on film. Impossible to deny.

I admit it. I thought submitting my rather strong will right from the get-go would send the wrong message. I wasn't passive. I was confidently assertive. I always resented the term "weaker sex" because I wasn't about to be. When our minister tied it into our marriage blessing, I did not consider it a pleasant serendipity.

How serendipitous indeed, because it has been a stabilizing rock in our marriage! I've learned that submission doesn't mean one of us is to be superior and the other inferior. It means that to have a healthy relationship, we must both be willing to go the extra mile, not because we *must*, but because we *want* to please our spouse even more

> Submission is a willing adaption; a voluntary selflessness to please God and to obey His Word.
>
> *Cynthia Heald*[4]

than ourselves. It is based on Christ's example of unconditional love which means kindness is extended even though it is not always deserved.

When I reflect over the last fifteen years, it is our mutual submission that has kept us in love more than anything else. But it didn't just happen. It became our mutual inner resolve to 1) follow God's principles for marriage and 2) to work on it daily.

The principle of submission comes from Ephesians 5:22: "Wives, submit to your husbands as to the Lord."

Cynthia Heald writes,

> God has asked us, as wives, to submit to a man we chose and most likely did our best to attract. As Christian wives in today's world—which idealizes the independent, self-oriented woman—we must do our best to consider biblical submission in depth.[5]

Submission is not strictly for the woman. In verse 25, God says, "Husbands, love your wives, just as Christ loved the church and gave himself up for her."

If our job of submitting to our husband is a difficult one, the husband's is even more so, because he is to suffer for his wife as Christ did for the Church. Many of us wives have made sure of that!

The problem is that we've made submission an unpleasant place to be because we don't handle it wisely. We lord it over each other and make it miserable. God meant for it to be mutually beneficial, a tool to help us get along with each other.

Ecclesiastes 4:9-10 says,

> Two are better than one,
>   because they have a good return for their work:
> If one falls down,
>   his friend can help him up.
> But pity the man who falls
>   and has no one to help him up!

Still not convinced that submission will make your marriage better? Afraid to give in? Consider the lesson from the next story.

Why It Works

Have you ever been in a three-legged race? Two people stand side by side. Their legs next to each other are tied together so they have only one free leg. The tied legs must move precisely at the same time or both people will fall when they begin to run.

We played this game one spring when we were at our friend's house along with about twenty other people. Needless to say, we bit the dust more than once because we were not in sync as a team. The more we tried to strong-leg the other person or pull away, the more we would fall.

"Laurie, speed up! Speed up!" Mike yelled.

"I can't speed up! You slow down!" And down we would tumble.

After several unsuccessful attempts, we realized if we moved as one unit, it was easier to move together in synchronous rhythm. First, we stood closer together, almost adjoined at the hip. Second, we put our arms around each other's waists and held on tight. Third, we became more willing to accommodate each other. (He slowed down and, what do you know, I had it in me to speed up.) The results were predictable. We stopped falling so much and had a lot more fun. And when we did fall,

> Love is not a feeling, but a choice.

> ... This kind of love is not emotional. One does not fall into and then out of this kind of love. It is a love of the will. It is something addressed to our volition. We do it because we make ourselves do it. We order ourselves. Because of Christ, we are motivated to love. We do not wait for attraction or like interests.
> *Arthur H. DeKruyter*[6]

we didn't cast blame. We just helped each other up, stayed close and held on tight.

That is how submission works. It is mutual cooperation. It is thinking of ways you can meet your spouse's needs. It is essential for marital success because it perpetuates oneness.

Submission works because it is God's plan for the marriage. Before He admonishes the women and men separately, in Ephesians 5:21 God says, "Submit to one another out of reverence for Christ." Notice that didn't say, "when you feel like it . . . ," "when you have extra time . . . ," "when your spouse deserves it. . . ." It commands it for the sake of Christ!

When a command is given in the military, it is not open for discussion—discussion is not an option. Can you imagine an enlisted soldier telling a general that he'll think about what he proposed and if he feels like it, he'll comply? Of course it's absurd. But isn't that what we do with God's commands when we don't follow them wholeheartedly? By not submitting, aren't we really saying, "I like my way better, God. I think I know what is best for me. In other words, God, You are wrong."

The marital message from the world is to be strong, make your own decisions and stay independent, but that is not God's plan for us. His best for us is a healthy marriage that makes one from two and that requires submission.

How to Show It

Perhaps a better definition of submission is respect. Humble respect leads us to consider others before ourselves. Philippians 2:3 says, "Do nothing out of selfish ambition or vain conceit, but in humility consider others better than yourselves."

That means there is no room for self-centeredness. Submission allows us to esteem our spouse and show him or her constant consideration, regardless of mood. Humble respect frees us to apologize first after an argument, regardless of the other person's attitude. When thoughtfulness and humility are combined, you have a love relationship that cannot be shaken.

Three examples of how Mike and I show our submission to each other are:

1. *Finances*—we never make a major purchase (for us that means over $100) without first discussing it and coming to a mutual agreement. Even if you find a "great deal" and purchase something you both will use, if your spouse doesn't agree with the purchase, then neither does God, no matter how much sense it makes to you. Using the same checking account is important because it demands detailed communication and accountability. To move more toward unity than independence, neither of us can be autonomous.

2. *Thoughtfulness*—we try to be considerate even when it isn't convenient. Mike is a bona fide morning person and likes to start his day early, as in 5 a.m. He likes it when I get up so we can chat before he leaves for work. After fifteen years, it's still a struggle because I'm a night owl. But usually I find myself crawling out of my warm covers to meet this very simple, but important, need simply because it pleases him. That is a form of submission.

Similarly, Mike knows how terrified I am to drive on the snow since I totaled my car a few winters ago. If the roads are bad, he will take his lunch hour to come home and run me safely on my errands, or he'll call me to get a grocery list and do the running for me. His business keeps him very busy through the day and it would be easy for him mentally to focus just on his work. To meet my needs when he is pulled in every direction from work is another form of submission.

I love the insights from Gary Chapman in *The Five Languages of Love*. He has discovered through twenty years of marriage counseling that there are five basic "love languages." Out of the five, we speak one primary language. That is how we most feel loved and also how we are most apt to show our love to others. The five languages are:

1. affirming words
2. quality time
3. receiving gifts
4. acts of service
5. physical touch.[7]

Mike's primary love language is acts of service, which explains why early in our marriage he would always fix me something to eat after an argument. I used to think, *Who can eat at a time like this? Why would you waste your time fixing this?* He did it because that is his love language. That was his way of being thoughtful, of submitting, of waving a white flag. It is his way of loving, but not mine.

> My heart is ever at your service.
>
> *William Shakespeare*

My primary love language is affirming words. Mark Twain once said, "I can live for two months on a good compliment." I would have to agree. Affirming words that come in the form of compliments, encouragement, kind words, humble words, meaningful conversation mean the world to me.

While I've learned to appreciate Mike's kind acts of service toward me, he has also learned that loving words are the most powerful way to show me thoughtfulness. He buys meaningful cards or writes his own; he calls through the day to say he loves me or appreciates something I've done; he keeps in tune with my projects and encourages me to finish strong; he has learned my love language and speaks it fluently.

Because his language is acts of service, I've made a list on my daily calendar of thoughtful ways I can help him. Most things on the list have been mentioned by him in the past as being very special and meaningful. They include:

- washing his back in the shower
- giving him a long back rub with lotion
- helping him with a project on the house (although I'm totally useless when it comes to nails, hammers and caulk). Being at his side to hand him these things makes his day.
- mowing the lawn in the summer (he's a golf course superintendent, so the last thing he wants to see when he comes

> One of the greatest ministries a wife can have in her husband's life is the ministry of encouragement through admiration. Not flattery, but sincere praise.
>
> *Carole Mayhall*[8]

> It works in this way—if we love a human being and do not love God, we demand of him every perfection and every rectitude, and when we do not get it we become cruel and vindictive;
>
> *(Continued on page 49.)*

home is more grass) even though it's not typically a female responsibility. Also, since I'm a Master Gardener (a certification program through the University of Illinois), I design the flower beds at his golf course every summer and help plant over 6,000 flowers—for free. Being able to relieve some of his stress at work gives me more fulfillment than any paycheck ever could. It is thoughtfulness that makes him feel important.

There are definitely differences in what we enjoy receiving from each other. Part of the fun and satisfaction of thoughtfulness is finding out what love language your spouse speaks. When you discover what it is, lavish it intentionally, generously and wholeheartedly.

3. *Intimacy*—again, it's knowing exactly what your mate likes. If you don't know, make it a point to find out.

We date at least once a week and that often includes a meal. He knows how much I enjoy the ambiance of our local Christian coffeehouse, Jitters and Rush, which is set in the downtown area with the original architecture from 100 years ago. They have cozy sofas, with dim lights and Pachelbel's *Canon* in D playing in the background.

He would much prefer to get in and out of a restaurant—a burger at Steak 'n Shake and he's out of there. But he always offers to take me to Jitters because he knows I find it romantic.

When we get home late and tuck the kids in bed, I may be totally exhausted and completely out of the mood, but I slip into a nightie that says "I'm interested" because it's important to him.

Submission is the most sublime of all the marital disciplines because it makes you want to treat your spouse like your best friend. And that is what you become.

Respectful Communication

All right. Perhaps you've been thinking, "I would submit to my husband (or wife) . . . if he (or she) weren't such a jerk!" I'm not suggesting that we are Ward and June Cleaver, never getting upset or angry with each other. I have a tendency to slam doors and raise my voice. The first year we were married we argued a lot. As a matter of fact, it got to the point when I was upset with him that I would go around and shut all the windows before the argument even began because I knew it was going to be loud and long.

Mike is the other extreme—although he's been known to yell, he is more apt to clam up and give an icy, cold shoulder. The only thing that brings us to our senses and budges us off our polar caps when we cool off is respect for the Word of God.

> we are demanding of a human being that which he cannot give. There is only one Being who can satisfy the last aching abyss of the human heart, and that is the Lord Jesus Christ. *Oswald Chambers*[9]

Ephesians 4:29 says, "Do not let any unwholesome talk come out of your mouths, but only what is helpful for building others up according to their needs, that it may benefit those who listen." I shudder to think what my neighbors heard me say during those early years. And worse, what a terrible sound that must have been reaching all of heaven.

Because a marriage is, after all, an intimate friendship, all of the rules from the first chapter apply to it as well: Give encouragement, Invest time, Forgive completely and Talk less, listen more. Additionally, marriage is the creating of one heart, which is no small task given our bent toward sin and independence. Therefore we must establish new habits that encourage unity.

Public Speaking

Because I was so frequently embarrassed by degrading remarks as a child, I am supersensitive to them as an adult. As a matter of fact, I can't think of anyone who actually likes being insulted—particularly from a spouse and especially in public, where others are privy to the shot. Nor is it edifying for those on the sidelines who have to hear cynical and debasing words thrown back and forth between married individuals like a game of hot potato.

Mike and I were at a party a few months ago where it was obvious one couple was "not in sync." As we made small talk, they would take turns throwing sarcastic barbs at each other.

"Cindy, see if you can get the recipe for this crab salad. The one you made last night was barely edible. Even the dog spit it out."

En garde.

"I'm just trying to help you lose those twenty pounds you've put on, dear," Cindy retorted.

Touché.

Such attacks are lethal to the life of the marriage. It is not only disrespectful and immature to speak to your spouse in such a condescending way, but it also forms a pattern for communication that is hard to break. Instead of directly addressing your problems and disagreements in private, you release your pain through verbal jabs in the presence of others. No one wins when this happens. The people listening are, at the very least, embarrassed and perhaps even appalled. Not only have you added salt to the wound in your spouse, but you have also created a negative impression of yourself to those within earshot. Your reputation can't help but fall a notch.

Practice Makes Perfect

So how do we communicate respect and honor in the presence of others? The answers are simple to give but may take some practice to incorporate. Here are our top five tips on how to achieve respectful communication:

1. *Respect yourself.* Even if you are starting at ground level, trying to break harmful communication habits toward your spouse, have enough respect for yourself to keep your mouth shut! In short, criticism makes *you* look worse than the person you're attacking, and you'll be remembered for your lack of social grace.
2. *It isn't funny or cute.* Making a joke doesn't make your jab hurt less. A punch to the stomach with a smile on your face is still a punch. Your spouse should never, ever be the butt of your joke, even if it is told in his or her absence. Use your own weaknesses and mistakes for the punch line, not your spouse's.
3. *Apply the Golden Rule.* "Do unto others as you would want them to do to you," is golden for a reason. We have high standards for how we want our spouse to treat us. If we would live by those

same standards, our spouse would feel like royalty. Keep that in mind the next time you are tempted to take the low road.
4. *Keep silent.* Apply the rule your mother gave you: "If you can't say something nice, don't say anything at all." Shouldn't we as intelligent, educated human beings, be able to control ourselves? Proverbs 10:19 says, "He who holds his tongue is wise." Conversely then, a person who cannot hold his tongue must be a fool. Don't prove it; keep silent.
5. *Practice, practice, practice.* Complimenting your spouse in public may not come naturally at first, but the more you do it, the easier it will be.

Start with common courtesy. Look for ways to appreciate your mate for what he or she *does*. Wives, thank your husbands for always taking out the garbage and mowing the lawn (or whatever it is you appreciate). Husbands, thank your wives for working so hard around the house and spending money wisely. Then work up to complimenting each other's character, who he or she *is*, in front of others.

Last month we attended our neighborhood picnic and met several new neighbors. One well-dressed man who appeared to be in his fifties or early sixties made a lasting impression on us. He recently married a woman well-known in our community and I asked him how they met.

"I was married for twenty-five years to a wonderful woman who was the light of my life. She passed away three years ago and I've never experienced such loneliness. When Judy walked into my office for some financial planning a year later, we talked for two hours and became instant friends. We've hardly been apart since. She thoroughly delights me and she is every bit as wonderful as she seems. She is the real deal and I couldn't be happier."

Mike and I both agreed that conversation was the highlight of the evening. To hear a man speak so well of his wife, to cherish her in front of people he hardly knew, warmed us to the bone. I can guarantee you he did not marry someone perfect, but he had disciplined himself to genuinely think of her that way and speak only good of her. We should be so inspired.

Winston Churchill once attended a formal banquet in London, where the dignitaries were asked the question, "If you could not be who you are, who would you be?"

Naturally, everyone was curious as to what Churchill, who was seated next to his beloved Clemmie, would say. After all, Churchill could not be expected to say Julius Caesar or Napoleon. When it finally came Churchill's turn, he rose and gave his answer. "If I could not be who I am, I would most like to be . . . Lady Churchill's second husband."[10]

Could he have said anything more brilliant? Certainly not in Clemmie's eyes.

Praising your spouse in public will strengthen your marriage and is a healthy habit we can all get better at with practice. But sometimes respectful communication is found in what we *don't* say.

Three years ago, when we were building our home, several of our friends were helping us finish the painting. We had only a few days before

> Scripture describes a giving love—a love that says, "Whatever I have, I want to share with you, and I want you to be what God meant you to be." It is a love that takes first things first as far as the other person is concerned.

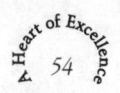

we were scheduled to close at the bank, so we were all working frantically to finish on time.

In the midst of that, Mike yelled to me from the top of the steps, as if I were three blocks away, to bring him more paint. There was more than a little frustration in his tone, and I could sense the impatience in his words. Instead of ordering him to pipe down or get it himself, after years of practicing verbal respect, I simply replied, "OK, hon, I'll be right there." Later he apologized for getting upset, and it was forgotten.

A month later, while having dinner with my friend Sarah, she commented how much she had appreciated the restraint I used during the painting incident. She thought it unusual that I hadn't yelled back, made a face behind his back or called him a name (I wish I could say I've *never* done that), and she thanked me for being an example to her.

That was a milestone for me because Mike is usually so much better at controlling his tongue than I am. It's a rare moment when I get to be the one to show restraint, but I was glad Sarah was there to see it!

Kind words about your spouse make you look good too. They also influence others to raise the bar for respectful communication in their own relationship.

How high is the bar in your marriage?

Passion

Heart-throbbing, earth-moving passion is a choice of your will. It is the eagerness to cause exhilaration and the insatiable desire to please your mate sexually and nonsexually. It may come in the form of a back rub at the kitchen table, a kiss on the neck while you watch the news, a lingering full body hug as you pass in the hallway or a thrilling night of lovemaking behind a closed door. Passion is the zeal to meet the needs of your mate. And it deepens in intensity when coupled with submission and respectful communication.

The problem is that most couples don't understand what it takes to maintain passion after the honeymoon is over, after the newness wears off and love isn't blind anymore. As a matter of fact, it doesn't take long at all to see with twenty-twenty vision how incredibly needy your mate is.

Willard Harley states in *His Needs, Her Needs* that most marital breakups occur when one or both partners lack the skills or awareness to meet each other's needs. The good news is that retraining is possible at any time. We're not born knowing how to please each other. It takes work and time to figure it out. But when our attitudes are right, when we embrace learning new skills, meeting our spouse's needs is never far behind. In other words, a willing attitude is the beginning of passion and must come before the action.

According to Harley, men and women have five basic needs. The top one for men is sexual fulfillment (followed by recreational companionship, attractive spouse, domestic support, admiration). For women, it's affection (followed by conversation, honesty, financial support, family commitment).[11]

Did you notice that none of the basic needs were the same? The man rates sex first but the

> The art of being wise is the art of knowing what to overlook.
>
> *William James*

woman doesn't even mention it. The woman rates affection first, and the man says, "So did I!" We are at opposite ends of the spectrum, to be sure, but that doesn't mean the needs are wrong. Because we are so different, most of the information I'll present is for sexual passion—what enhances and inhibits it.

I'm reminded of the couple who went to a marriage counselor to resolve some sexual issues. The counselor asked the woman to explain the problem and she said. "We have sex constantly, three times a week." The husband also explained the problem: "We never have sex. It's only three times a week."

Suffice it to say we are wired differently with a similar problem. We expect to have our own way.

A woman told me a few years ago that her husband just didn't get it. "Why can't he understand that I need a mood, a certain setting to prepare myself emotionally for intimacy?"

"What kind of setting do you mean? Do you need soft music playing on the stereo, several candles lit in the bedroom, the sheets pulled back neatly with a rose on the pillow and a note of sweet affection on the night stand?"

"Exactly." And she threw her hands up as if to say, "Finally, someone understands!"

"So, if you don't mind me asking, how long has it been since you've been 'in the mood'?"

"A couple of months, I guess. It feels like forever."

When I speak at conferences I always make time to counsel one-on-one because people are desperate for answers. If they weren't, they wouldn't be telling a complete stranger such intimate details. When it comes to intimacy, the stories may vary a little but they all have a common thread: women complain that their husbands lack tender affection but then smother them with sexual advances, and it's never romantic enough. Men complain that their wives are overweight, and that it's just not often enough.

To both I offer a profound suggestion: *Get real!* Until you do get real, you'll always think in the back of your mind, *If my spouse really loved me, he/she would make me feel like it. I guess we're just not compatible. If I'd only married the right person, I'd feel the way I'm supposed to feel.* Listen: if you wait for perfect emotions to lead you into this blissful state, you will have to wait forever. Chances are your spouse doesn't resemble Barbie or Ken, and there just isn't always time to pander to your every whim. Rick Warren, pastor of Saddleback Church in Orange County, California, said there are two laws to marriage:

1. You married an imperfect person.
2. You're not so hot yourself.

The only thing that will ever be perfect in your marriage, including your intimacy, is the God who created it. Accept that and we can move forward. To pine away for a Hollywood illusion, much less demand it, will drain the life right out of your marriage.

So how do we get so sidetracked? Why are there such long lapses in between visits to paradise? Very simply, we stop pursuing it. We stop making it a habit. Other responsibilities get in the way (raising kids, long work hours, overcommitted schedules, etc.) and our marital health loses its rightful position of second place (God first). We pass each other like platonic roommates, and the intense pleasure we experienced on our honeymoon is a distant memory.

But a marriage that is missing sexual passion is not abiding under God's rules. First Corinthians 7:3-5 says:

> The husband should fulfill his marital duty to his wife, and likewise the wife to her husband. The wife's body does not belong to her alone but also to her husband. In the same way, the husband's

body does not belong to him alone but also to his wife. Do not deprive each other.

Passion was God's idea, and it is part of His perfect plan for your marriage. If you doubt that, you've never read Song of Solomon. Here are a few excerpts:

> How beautiful you are, my darling!
>> Oh, how beautiful!
>> Your eyes are doves.
>
> How handsome you are, my lover!
>> Oh, how charming! (1:15-16)

> You have stolen my heart
>> with one glance of your eyes. (4:9)

> His mouth is sweetness itself;
>> he is altogether lovely.
> This is my lover, this my friend. (5:16)

You get the picture.

Herbert Miles writes, "God created this one-flesh experience to be the most intense height of physical intimacy and the most profound depth of spiritual oneness between husband and wife."[12] It obviously pleases God when we feel such fervor for our mate or it wouldn't have been included in the Bible. And you can bet it pleases your mate to be the recipient of such intense passion.

Wives, we can do better. It's wrong to make our husbands beg for sexual fulfillment. It makes them feel unloved and rejected. When women ask me how often is reasonable, I give them Dr. James Dobson's advice: every two to three days as a general guideline, with room for every couple to agree on specifics. If they balk at the idea of that often, I remind them that we are not to "withhold" due to selfishness or laziness, and that lack of sexual fulfillment is the primary reason men have affairs. They cannot be rewired (trust me, I tried); therefore it is our responsibility to learn to meet their needs.

Husbands, we desperately need you to touch us without an ulterior motive. Hold our hand while we walk, stroke our hair while we sit, rub our backs (and only our backs), kiss us tenderly through the day, cuddle us during a movie, put an arm around us at church, etc. We are wired to receive tenderness. If it isn't there, your sexual advances will make us resentful. Lack of affection, according to Willard Harley, is the number one reason women have affairs. Therefore, it is your responsibility to touch us unselfishly.

Mike and I have incredible passion in our marriage but it has not come without a struggle. It's been difficult for both of us to accept that our needs are completely different, and to be passionate about meeting those needs when we may feel slighted. But what always brings us back to the center is taking our eyes off of "me" and focusing on "us."

Passion is truly a choice, a matter of the will, but along the way Mike and I noticed that certain situations made that choice easier, while others made it seem more like work. So we came up with a list of practical habits that have helped tremendously. If these don't seem to fit your marriage, then make up your own list of helpful habits or ones you'd like to try.

Physically

1. *Groom impeccably*

I know this should go without saying, but shower and shave every day, twice a day if needed. Guys, even if you work at home, shower first thing in the morning and put on some cologne. I love it when Mike is clean, smooth and smelling good, and he has learned that he likes me to like it! If you're not used to this habit, the first few times your wife may ask where you're going. You shouldn't look and smell better for your coworkers and clients than you do for your precious wife. Make a regular habit out of looking your best for her so she doesn't have to wonder what is up when you do.

I teach an exercise class where the average age is eighty. The senior citizens come to class dressed as if they were going downtown. One eighty-four-year-old gentleman, in particular, always wears a neatly pressed shirt, shiny shoes and a hint of cologne. When I commented about his wonderful appearance, he quipped, "A man with my potential must be prepared at all times." His wife giggled approvingly. Men, are you doing all you can to present yourself at your best to your wife? What grooming habits need to be upgraded?

Women, if you work at home as a full-time homemaker or do business from home, make sure you do your hair and makeup first thing in the morning as if you were going out. Not only is it more appealing to our husbands, but you'll also find it puts you in a better mood, more open to being friendly, fun and sensual.

Another habit that Mike appreciates from me is shaving my legs every day. I really don't like doing it so I tried to get out of it, at least that often. I whittled it down to twice a week hoping Mike wouldn't notice. He noticed and then asked how I would like it if he came to bed with whiskers on his cheeks. Point taken. I would have voiced the same complaint so I'm back to every day.

We would never let our partner see us unkempt when we were dating; should they see any less now? When we were trying to attract them during the courtship, no amount of work was too much if it pleased them. Falling in love was easy because we were so conscientious. Don't let laziness prevail. Take the extra step to look, feel and smell luscious all the time because meticulous grooming is a habit that makes passion easier.

2. Stay fit

If you've gotten away from an exercise program, get back to it. You owe it to yourself and your partner to be as healthy and fit as possible. Fitness increases your energy and gives you emotional reserves for when you and your loved one are finally alone. Being fit gives you more confidence to leave the lights on. How can you be fully uninhibited sexually if you are worried about how you look? Being fit also raises your self-esteem, and while it won't necessarily give you a perfect body, you are more apt to realize that you don't have to have a hot body to have a hot attitude.

3. Dress to please

I'm always cold, so to trade my long underwear for a thin, silky nightie is a great sacrifice. It's worth it, though, because—let's face it—men are visual creatures.

Ladies, how long has it been since you've bought new sleepwear? (Why do they call it that, anyway? Nobody ever sleeps in that stuff!) Are you wearing underclothing that is losing its elastic or has fading color? Buy what you know will please your husband—which is not always completely comfortable or practical. Buy it anyway. It's a great investment for renewing the passion. (For warmth, we can buy flannel sheets.)

Men, what is your wife's favorite color or material on you? Is there a particular style of clothing she likes to see you in?

Mike is one handsome guy. I especially like to see him in a tie, so whenever we go out to a nice dinner, he'll GQ-it-up for me. I know he's more comfortable in a golf shirt and dockers, but it's his little sacrifice to bring me pleasure. Couple that with his cologne and smooth cheeks, and my hairless legs and uncomfortable undergarments, and we are off to a sizzling start!

We are different! Men like to see their wives in next to nothing, women tend to enjoy seeing their husbands fully clothed. Let's accept that and do our best to please each other.

Emotionally

1. Get to know him/her

Part of the beauty of passion is that it is not always one-size-fits-all. Knowing your spouse—what hurts, what brings joy, what knocks his or her socks off—can only be achieved from conversation. This kind of conversation leads to greater understanding and intimacy. So why don't we do it more often? Probably the greatest enemy of intimacy is materialism. It has been called "the great American scramble for more goodies,"[14] but the price we pay is way too high. The more we want, the more we have to work; the more time we spend purchasing, the less time we have to get to know each other. I'm convinced that God designed us so that it would take a lifetime to really know each other. But how can we continually learn about our mate if conversation isn't a part of our daily habits?

Richard Swenson, author of *The Overload Syndrome*, states: "The contemporary American axiom is to maximize everything. We spend ten percent more than we have whether it's time,

> For the tongue is a pen, which, pressing deeply enough (and whether for good or for evil), will write upon the heart.
>
> *Mike Mason*[13]

money, or energy. We work hard, play hard, and crash hard."[15]

It seems the only thing we aren't maximizing is communication with our spouses. But how can we when we are in the midst of a hyperliving lifestyle? Even the best counselor in the world cannot fix a marriage with only fifteen minutes of conversation.

If we do not focus, life will "just happen" to us. It is up to us to save our marriages, and the only way to do that is by spending time getting to know our spouses and how to please them.

How often do you and your spouse take a quiet moment to sit and chat? Could you answer some basic questions about their likes and dislikes?

- If he didn't have to work, how would he spend his time?
- Where in the world would she most like to travel?
- What is his favorite current song? Group?
- What is her favorite childhood memory?
- What is her greatest regret about her education?
- What would he most like to be remembered for?
- What is he fearful of?
- What is her favorite way to be kissed?

> It is a foolish woman who expects her husband to be to her that which only Jesus Christ Himself can be: always ready to forgive, totally understanding, unendingly patient, invariably tender and loving, unfailing in every area. . . . Such expectations put a man under an impossible strain.
>
> *Ruth Bell Graham*[16]

Could you answer all of those? Could you answer any? Part of what brings us to oneness is knowing and being known. That only happens by constant, intentional conversation. You be the one to pursue these answers. Don't wait for the other person to ask. Lead the way in engaging conversation about the other person (remember Talk less; listen more?).

The more we invest our time in knowing each other, the greater our passion will be. First, because we'll feel more loved, and second, because we'll know how to love better.

2. Speak love

Florence Littauer said, "If you want heaven at 11, start at 7." I'm sure she meant 7 a.m. so that you can use the entire day as an aphrodisiac. Kind words of encouragement, gentle words of understanding, whispered words of appreciation sprinkled throughout the day are verbal foreplay. They enhance the emotional passion you feel for your mate, which almost always spills over into the physical. And when you invest words of love into your marriage, they come back to you with interest.

3. Think love

It's so important to take every thought captive, as it says in Second Corinthians 10:5. What makes our thoughts important is that they determine how we act. If we are thinking critically about our mate with thoughts like, *He is so self-centered; Boy, is she out of shape; If he weren't so lazy, we'd have more money,* then we are less likely to be loving to them. But if we are controlling our thoughts and training them to be pure and optimistic, then we will have an insatiable desire to meet the needs of our spouse. Our thoughts will motivate us either to criticize them unfairly and withhold love or to believe the best in them, withholding nothing.

Conclusion

Submission, respectful communication and passion are three guidelines that will move us toward oneness and away from separateness. Every day we must intentionally choose them because they will never just happen. If we wholeheartedly pursue these habits that help us live by God's rules, then our marriages will flourish. If we don't, they won't. It's as simple and as difficult as that.

This meshing together stuff sure is hard. Creating one heart out of two imperfect ones is certainly beyond any of us. That's why we need a divine set of rules and a divine Savior to keep us on the right path. After all, who better to help us die to ourselves than the One who died for us? Yes, against the odds I want my marriage to be thrilling, to dwell among the twenty-five percent who are making it, and to be a sweet aroma to all who are touched by it. And I know this one secret: with God as the center, it will be.

Discussion Questions

1. In which of the three areas—submission, respectful communication, passion—would the health of your marriage rate the highest? What healthy habits reflect your efforts to meet your mate's needs?
2. What's something that your spouse has repeatedly asked you to do but you have refused? Would it glorify God for you to do it?
3. What is your spouse's love language (words of affirmation, quality time, gifts, touch, service)? Is it different from yours? What is one habit you can begin this week to start speaking it? (If your mate's language is words, how can you encourage, praise and

compliment him or her? If it is service, how can you serve? If gifts, what can you purchase or make? If time, what would he or she enjoy doing with you? If touch, does he or she like back rubs?) Would your spouse think you were being "thoughtful" if you did this?
4. How can Philippians 2:3 make your marriage stronger? Memorize this passage together.
5. Because a lasting marriage is built by small daily habits, what is one thing you can stop doing that hurts your marriage? What is one thing you can begin doing or do more consistently that will help it?

Endnotes

1. Stephen T. Wyatt, *Behind the Tent Flaps* (Joplin, MO: College Press Publishing Company, 1997), p.11.

2. Dawn Bradley Berry, *Divorce Recovery* (Los Angeles: Lowell House, 1998), p. ix.

3. Willard F. Harley, Jr., *His Needs, Her Needs* (Grand Rapids, MI: Revell, 1994), p. 44.

4. Cynthia Heald, *Loving Your Husband* (Colorado Springs: NavPress, 1989), p. 68.

5. Ibid., p. 62.

6. Arthur H. DeKruyter, in J. Allan Petersen, ed., *Family Concern*, vol. 10, no. 3 (1986), quoted in Heald, p. 60.

7. Gary Chapman, *The Five Languages of Love* (Chicago: Northfield Publishing, 1995), p. 15.

8. Carole Mayhall, "Choosing to Admire," in Jack and Carole Mayhall, *Marriage Takes More Than Love* (Colorado Springs: NavPress, 1978), p. 150.

9. Oswald Chambers, *My Utmost for His Highest* (New York: Dodd, Mead & Co., 1935), p. 212.

10. James Humes, *Churchill, Speaker of the Century* (Briarcliff Manor, NY: Stein and Day, Scarborough House, 1980), p. 291, as quoted in R. Kent Hughes, *Disciplines of a Godly Man* (Wheaton, IL: Crossway Books, 1991), p. 44.

11. Harley, p. 63.

12. Herbert J. Miles, *Sexual Happiness in Marriage* (Grand Rapids: Zondervan, 1967), p. 28.

13. Mike Mason, *The Mystery of Marriage* (Portland, OR: Multnomah Press, 1985), p. 67.

14. Harley, p. 13.

15. Richard A. Swenson, *The Overload Syndrome* (Colorado Springs: NavPress, 1988), p. 15.

16. Ruth Bell Graham, *It's My Turn* (Old Tappan, NJ: Revell, 1982), p. 74.

Chapter 3

Parenting: A Heart's Legacy

More important than the financial inheritance we leave our children is the legacy of our character. Who we are and how we are known is largely a result of choices. First we make choices, then our choices make us, a little bit at a time. If we can learn to establish daily habits born of wise choices that reflect goodness, sound judgment, acceptance and wisdom, then our children will grow up knowing they are loved, enabling them to make their own wise and good choices. Those are the true riches we bequeath because they leave our future generations an example to follow and a powerful reminder of what we chose to value.

Mike's grandparents died sixteen years ago and left us a generous gift from their estate. But what is a more lasting treasure are the ways they touched the lives of their children and grandchildren. Since I was never able to meet them, I cherish the stories Mike and his family tell. Some memories are funny. Some are poignant. A few are sad. But all are special because they leave us a legacy of love with which to fill our hearts.

Mike's grandparents, Frank and Lucille, were married sixty-one years. Their marriage survived the Depression, two world wars, an entire year apart when Frank was hospitalized for blood poisoning, unemployment and the struggle to make ends meet with four children to support. Through every crisis they stayed together, held on to their faith, and by helping each other, grew stronger in themselves. Their four children grew up, married and established their own strong families built on the same principles: faith, love and commitment. At family reunions their grandchildren recite story after story of fun and memorable times spent in Frank and Lucille's backyard playing. They knew they were loved, and they knew beyond a doubt that their grandparents loved each other.

I guess that love and how they grew to live with "one heart" was never more vividly displayed than in their deaths. They both died on the same day, August 17, just before noon, exactly one year apart. Frank died of a heart attack, and the next year Lucille died of a broken one.

Mike's parents (his mom is Frank and Lucille's only daughter) celebrated their fiftieth anniversary just a few months ago. What a tender and moving experience to see them recommit their vows to each other in the same church in which they were married. The fiftieth must be called golden for how it makes their children feel—rich beyond measure.

Mike's oldest brother Jim gave an appropriate speech at their anniversary dinner. "Mom and Dad," he began, "they say the greatest gift parents can give their children is to love each other. Thank you for giving us that gift, for living by your promises to love for better or worse, in hard times and good, for fifty glorious years. You have given us a gift that is truly priceless."

Amen!

My mom and dad had been married thirty years when Dad died at the young age of fifty-two. Even though I didn't feel close to him (our relationship was always strained), it gave me great joy and security to see him and my mother together and committed to one another. Unfortunately, he died before I could tell him how important that was to me.

When we appreciate and honor our parents we please God. After all, it was His idea. In Ephesians 6:1-3 we are admonished:

> Children, obey your parents in the Lord, for this is right. "Honor your father and mother"—which is the first commandment with a promise—"that it may go well with you and that you may enjoy long life on the earth."

Not only is it a good idea but it is a commandment. That means if we don't do it, we are sinning. It's not just being distant or neglectful—call it busyness or sugarcoat it any way you want, but it doesn't change what it really is to God—it is sin.

But what are we to do when we don't feel close to them, when memories from our parents are not dear? How should we respond when the legacy we've been left is embarrassing or traumatic or too tainted by pain to remember any good?

Are there painful childhood (or even adult) memories that keep you from forgiving your parents? Is there a traumatic memory of neglect or abuse locked so far down inside your heart that it keeps you from appreciating any good they have given you? If you are having trouble honoring, appreciating and loving your parents and in-laws in such a way that pleases the Lord, then you need to search your heart and find out what is wrong.

Could you have inadvertently done or said something to upset them and now there is distance in your relationship? Could there be something you are holding against them but you're not quite sure

> A parent's love is more important to a child than wealth or education or any form of material possession.
>
> Tim LaHaye

what it is? Maybe you do know what it is, but it has such a strong grip on your emotions that you can't let it go.

I'm not talking about the kind of mistakes that send parents to prison or cause children to be taken away from them. I mean the kind of unintentional mistakes, the subtle misunderstandings, the lack of involvement, the verbal digs in public, the small human errors that can separate us forever emotionally.

What I've discovered about parents' mistakes is that you must forgive them if you want peace in your life. Every corner of your heart must be cleaned out, leaving no room for grudges and bitterness, or that will be the legacy you pass on to your own children. Just as parents leave a legacy with their choices, as children we also leave a legacy with how we choose to love our parents.

That is not always easy. As a matter of fact, sometimes it may seem flat-out impossible, but God did not decipher between perfect and imperfect parents when He commanded us to honor them. Sometimes cleaning out the corners where there is disappointment, rejection and mistakes can cause some emotional turmoil and make the pain temporarily worse. Tears may come uncontrollably. Your anger may flare. You may need to grieve. But in the end, if you can forgive and let go of your parents' mistakes, you'll be more at peace with yourself and freer to love and honor them.

Parenting: A Heart's Legacy

A few months ago, our good friend, Steve, shared some of his most vivid childhood memories during our small group church meeting. Steve loved baseball and was an all-star Little Leaguer. Every week his dad would watch him play. But after the game, instead of going to the victory celebration at Dairy Queen with the rest of the team, his dad would haul him over to the local bar and buy him kiddie cocktails, while he would get drunk on beer.

Steve would play pinball all night—alone—until he was so exhausted he would go outside and fall asleep in the backseat of their car. His dad would leave the bar at 2 a.m. and drive them home, totally smashed, every week.

When Steve told us that story, my heart nearly broke in two. Not only was he deprived of a meaningful childhood memory, celebrating with his teammates, but he didn't get to celebrate with anyone! He was forced into the perversion of his father's world and wasn't allowed a word of complaint or given a promise for next time. He had to take it like a man—at the tender age of ten.

Steve shared that without a crack in his voice or a tear in his eye. I thought that a bit unusual considering the severity of the situation, but I assumed he must have worked through it already, having had over twenty years to grieve in private.

Several days later Steve confided to us that he had been severely depressed since the day he had shared his story, often missing work to stay home and cry, sometimes uncontrollably. And it further upset him that he couldn't identify anything traumatic enough in his life to cause such emotional upheaval. Work was going well, he and his wife were "in sync," life was good.

We mentioned his dad and asked Steve if he had ever grieved over the childhood situation with his father. He admitted he hadn't. He had locked away those memories and thrown away the key . . . until the night he had conveyed it to our small group. "I'm surprised I

> He who cannot forgive his parents burns the bridge over which he himself must cross.

shared that because it's usually just easier to pretend it never happened," he recalled. "I can't change it now, so why should I dredge it up?"

It must be brought to the forefront for the simple fact that sweeping a problem, a painful memory, a disappointment, under the rug doesn't get rid of it—it only makes it harder to walk. But once the problem is identified and you allow yourself to grieve over it, the healing can begin. Sometimes we can do that with friends, sometimes in private with our spouse. Other times we may need a professional Christian counselor to help us work through it.

If you find this is where you are, get help from someone you trust so you can work on letting go and getting on with your own healing. And if your relationship is estranged with your parents, don't let your own healing be contingent on reconciling with them. You can't control how they feel or what they say today, but you can keep the past from reigning over you now. Letting go will relieve you of a heavy burden and it might eventually give you a new appreciation for your parents.

Then again, some of us may find it easier to give forgiveness when we ourselves are in need of it from our own children. When we become parents, all of a sudden it is much easier to understand why ours failed. It's impossible to be perfect.

Choose One Word

While there are many areas of my childhood I wish I could change, I have learned, for my own emotional health and to be obedient to God, to dwell on my parents' strengths. An exercise that has helped me identify those is to choose one positive word to describe each of them. I had allowed my unbridled tongue to criticize and dishonor them for so many years, justifying it with examples of their inadequacies, that at first this exercise was very difficult. I had dwelt on their offenses so frequently that I'm now ashamed to say I had never really considered what was good.

But after making my mind up several years ago that I would obey God by honoring my parents and now my in-laws, practicing this exercise has made it easier. I can now identify obvious, even sacrificial ways they showed me love and how their character reflected strong family values, faith and commitment that was so often a trademark of their generation.

The word Mike and I chose for his dad was honesty. Mike remembers when he and his dad, Al, walked over a mile back to a store where the clerk had given Al too much change. It was only a few cents, but it was a principle his dad lived by—the principle of being honest at all times, even if it inconveniences you, embarrasses you or even if no one else is. Mike has never forgotten that powerful lesson, because his dad led by example.

For my dad, it would be generosity. I remember our pastor calling him and asking if he had some concrete blocks that he could give to a family with a flooded basement. They needed to fix their foundation so it would stay dry, but they didn't have enough money to purchase the materials. With five kids, money was tight at our house too, but my dad gave them at no charge all the blocks he had been saving for a project on our house, and even helped them with the work. We didn't get our project done for a long time after that, but now I realize we didn't go without.

For both of our mothers, the word that described their character would be devotion. They gave us the wonderful gift of being full-time homemakers so they could nurture us with the special love that only a mom can give. They could have worked outside the home and been able to give us more *things,* but they chose to give us the best thing—themselves. They received no pay for this very important job, but they have children who are eternally thankful and have continued the legacy they began.

What will be the one word your children use to describe you? What kind of legacy will your character leave indelibly etched on their hearts?

I can think of some words I hope my children use to describe me: loving, fun, devoted, gentle. But will my goodness be obvious? Will they remember the tender words spoken more than the impatient and critical? Am I leaving a void anywhere that will wound them? What habits am I establishing today that will shout loud and clear when they are grown, "You mattered to me!"?

While learning to be a more loving and obedient daughter and every day learning to "dwell on the good," I'm striving to improve my own parenting skills as well. Being halfway around the track with children aged nineteen, thirteen and ten, I have seen and experienced many things that worked well and plenty that didn't. I've concluded (and research seems to back it up) that kids have specific needs that cry out to be met. Just as adults need physical, emotional and spiritual nurturing to thrive, kids do too.

Physical Needs

The biggest part of parenting is meeting the needs of our children. More than anything, I want my children to remember that I made time to provide for their physical needs. I want them to know that I value them enough first to know their needs, and second, to work hard at taking care of them.

Not that I cater to their every whim so they develop into lazy sloths that demand service! I am responsible to care for them in such a way that they learn values and skills for someday taking care of their own families with the best that is in them. One day they will carry on the habits of a family meal, healthy sleep patterns and generous affection in their own families. Meeting these needs helps our children develop properly and makes them feel loved, accepted and cared for.

Meal Time

When I speak at conferences on the issue of nutrition, I'm amazed how far we've fallen. A generation ago, families came together in the evening for dinner and it was an event that no one missed. A "meat and potatoes" kind of meal was served, with a variety of vegetables, bread and fruit as side dishes. Sundays were reserved for a special meal with grandparents and extended family. But now it seems that in the 2000s, with a frantic pace of life, a nutritious meal that includes all the food groups and pulls the family together to share the events of the day is falling by the wayside. And we are not better for it.

> Pleasant words are a honeycomb, sweet to the soul and healing to the bones.
>
> Proverbs 16:24

> Be a mother. It's a rewarding thing. Mothers and Christmas are the two best things in the world.... But my mother is the best gift I ever got.
>
> Marie, age 9

Come on, parents, what has happened to us? Are we so busy that we can't sit down to a nutritious family meal anymore? I'm afraid we're missing out here, and not just on healthy food. In *The Disconnected Generation*, Josh McDowell, noted author and family expert, states:

> Parents, you may find that an excellent time to chat with your kids about their thoughts, feelings, and dreams is at dinnertime. Young people are usually more open to conversation during a meal. If you can get them to talk about the day's events, their feelings will probably rise to the surface as well.[1]

Kids need two things in this area: food that makes them healthy and strong, and what I call "face time" with the rest of the family. Face time is just as crucial as consuming the right foods because the soul is fed when the entire family sits down and converses about the day. It not only teaches greater social skills, but it also sends our children a message that they are valued, that their role in the family is significant and that their opinions and ideas matter.

This needs to happen as often as possible, hopefully three days each week or more. And while no hunger pangs signal this deprivation, it is a form of starvation just the same. Your children need to know they are important, and scheduling a mealtime where nutritious food is served and everyone's presence is required is a powerful way to communicate that. If your current schedule is keeping you from having a mealtime together several times a week, then let's examine what can be changed to accommodate it.

- If your children have activities after school, would it be possible to offer them an after-school snack (instead of hitting the drive-through) that would hold off their hunger until a later family dinner?
- Is it possible that your child simply has too many activities going at the same time? Try to prioritize activity choices and allow each child to choose only one per season.
- Does the idea of cooking that often seem daunting? If your children are old enough, involve them in the process. Have them choose recipes that are simple enough for them to help with.
- Do you have a crockpot cookbook? That will save your sanity during the 5 o'clock "arsenic hour," when everyone is hungry and cranky, anxious for the meal to be ready. You won't have to scurry around trying to throw something together because it will already be cooking.
- What about the weekends? If your schedule will absolutely not permit you to dine together through the week, choose either Saturday or Sunday night as your designated family meal and hold your ground. This is too important to give up on.

Sleep

My oldest son, David, and I were discussing the implications of napping and just how much sleep is enough. My position was that if you are sleeping deeply enough and long enough at night, you shouldn't need a nap. He had a clever comeback. "But, Mom," he argued, "if you're able to fall asleep—you're supposed to be!"

Very true, I had to admit. If your body didn't actually need rest for some reason, it would keep you awake.

Sleep deprivation in adults is not a pretty sight. It makes us cranky, impatient and hard to live with. But in children the ramifications are even more significant, because they need their rest for physical development. Our children's bodies are still developing into their early twenties, which is all the more reason to ensure they establish healthy sleeping habits early.

Here are some rules that will ensure a good night's sleep for everyone:

1. *Every child should sleep in his own bed.* From the time a baby is born, he should have his own sleeping quarters. That may mean in the same room while you are nursing, but it should still be separate beds. Babies who constantly sleep in their parents' bed become toddlers who are afraid to sleep alone. That hurts them *and* you.

2. *Have a set bedtime and a predictable routine.* Go to bed at the same time and get up at the same time every day. Firm rules in this area actually help children feel more secure because they know what to expect. An established, predictable routine helps children develop other great habits such as reading, praying and good hygiene. Our children fall asleep much quicker when they go through these steps every night. On the one or two nights a week when there is a sitter staying with them, they still maintain the routine, and that gives them a sense of normalcy even in our absence.

How much is enough? A study at the University of Chicago revealed that toddlers need about eleven hours a night, plus a two-hour nap (lucky ducks). Preschoolers should receive eleven to twelve hours of sleep each night with an afternoon rest period. A child in grade school needs ten hours of sleep each night, with an occasional catnap on weekends. Teenagers can require nine to ten hours, depending on their activity level.[2]

Yes, even though older children are closer to being adults, they are going through such dramatic developmental changes that they require a lot of sleep. They are not being lazy; their bodies need the extra rest to grow properly.

3. *Make their rooms warm and inviting, not stimulating media centers.* Kids these days have a ton of stuff—computers, video games, DVDs, TVs, phones, stereos. Be careful how many of these are allowed in the child's room. A bedroom is meant to be a place of rest, so try to limit the electronic toys and items that may keep them from some much-needed sleep. (Besides, do you really want your children to have unrestricted access to cable and the Internet?)

We keep our computer in the office (only Mike and I know the password), and the TV, DVDs and video games are all in the family room to encourage more face time. The only phone in a bedroom is ours. (They've come up with some brilliant reasons why they should have one too, but so far we've stood our ground.)

To add a little more warmth to your children's bedroom, try framing their favorite pictures from family vacations or other fun memories so they are surrounded by images of love and happiness. Even teenagers appreciate this. No matter how well-adjusted your children are, they need constant reminders of how loved they are. Make their room a happy and peaceful haven.

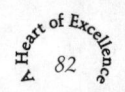

> Talk not of wasted affection. Affection was never wasted.
>
> *Henry Wadsworth Longfellow*

Affection

Children need a family mealtime. They need to sleep long enough and in a restful environment. And they need to receive affection in a way that nurtures their self-esteem and makes them feel cherished.

Whether it's a gentle touch on the arm or a passionate bear hug, it feels good to be touched. My friend Julie is a hugger. She isn't afraid to give me a full body hug and a kiss on the cheek when she hasn't seen me for a while. I don't think it strange or intrusive. She simply loves her friends and believes affection is a convincing way to show it. I admire her boldness to be so demonstrative. I have never left her presence without feeling a little more cheery and a little more loved.

Affection has the same effect on children. Even from birth, studies have recorded the dramatic effects of affection. Babies who were held, coddled and stroked developed healthier immune systems, stronger lungs and grew faster than babies who weren't. In fact, babies who were denied affection suffered numerous illnesses and showed profound setbacks in all areas of development.

Studies in state-run orphanages in Romania revealed that "persistent cognitive and emotional defects" occurred much more frequently in abandoned infants as compared to children in nurturing environments.[3]

Parenting: A Heart's Legacy

"Sometimes the best medicine is a hug," has been quoted by many, but now it appears to have some measurable validity. Researchers at Boston University instructed mothers to pick up their newborns and cuddle them for fifteen minutes before the babies were stuck with a needle to draw blood. Snuggled infants cried and grimaced much less than those who didn't get the soothing human contact.[4]

Lack of affection in childhood can impact adulthood as well. At John Hopkins University, medical doctors who graduated from 1948-1964 were tracked for several years. Researchers found that "lack of [physical and emotional] closeness with parents" was the only single common factor to hypertension, cardiovascular disease, mental illness and suicide.[5]

Affection, or lack of it, not only affects our children's health, but society as a whole. In *Becoming the Parent God Wants You to Be*, Kevin Leman cites a doctor who studied forty-nine different cultures throughout the world to determine what effect physical affection and touch have on children. He learned that the more violent societies were the ones in which touching and healthy caressing were rare in the family.[6]

Every child needs constant affection in his own way. It may be as subtle as a touch to the shoulder or as deliberate as holding our children in our arms or, if they are young, on our lap for hours on end. The effect is the same—they feel loved and important. Their hearts are comforted, inspired, reassured, encouraged, calmed and even cheered when we take time to reach out and show them a tender and thoughtful touch. And the need never goes away, even when they become taller than we are.

David, being almost twenty, obviously no longer wants to "cuddle" but loves to roughhouse and wrestle. Along with occasional quick hugs and shoulder rubs, this is the form of affection with

> Children need affection at every age, and if they don't get it, they will fulfill their need in the wrong way.
>
> *Josh McDowell* [7]

which he is most comfortable. This meets his affection needs while still respecting his personal space as a young adult.

Allie, at thirteen, loves to have her back rubbed at bedtime. She finds this so relaxing that she will often fall asleep in the midst of it. She also appreciates when I wake her in the morning by stroking her cheek and rubbing her head, and she always has time for a hug before she leaves for school. She needs the greatest amount of affection when she has some physical hurt. Affection for her soothes everything from a skinned knee to a broken heart.

When Evan was eight he would surprisingly still allow me to kiss his cheek in public and would jump into my arms for a big hug when I visited him during his school lunchtime. Now at ten, he's more apt to jump onto my back for a piggyback ride than to want a hug. And that is OK, because that's what his needs are.

Another very important time to give your children affection is at their sporting events or competitions. Whether it's a soccer game, spelling bee or chess match, children desperately need your touch during these anxious moments, even if it only lasts a second. It's so important to be there to give them a high five or to put a consoling arm around their shoulder when they're disappointed or injured.

No matter what form of affection your child enjoys the most, it all carries the same loving message: "You are important to me. I enjoy being with you, and I think you're wonderful. I love you."

When affections are showered on them the way they like it best, one of their most basic and important needs is wholly satisfied. When that is combined with a consistent family mealtime and uninterrupted sleep, they are well on their way to becoming healthy and vibrant adults, having never felt neglect or disappointment that their physical needs weren't met.

Emotional Needs

Emotional needs are tricky. When the body is hungry or tired, there are strong controls in the brain that sound an alert. Tummies growl, blood sugar levels drop and moods turn nasty; we yawn or just simply fall asleep. But there aren't any built-in regulators that immediately signal when there are unmet emotional needs. Kids trust us as their parents to say that which is true and to do what is best for them. Period. If we say it, they believe it. And how we spend our time speaks volumes to them about their importance.

How are we doing, parents? Do our children feel accepted for exactly who they are? Or do we criticize them because they are different from us? Are we carving out time to be with our kids and making them feel special? Or are they drawn to other families that take more of an interest in their activities? To err in the realm of emotional needs has lifelong consequences. Sometimes it is locked away like our friend Steve's was, but sometimes it sits on their shoulder for the whole world to see.

I first met Kim when she came into our health club and wanted to lose forty pounds. Actually, her doctor had ordered her to in an effort to bring down her high blood pressure and cholesterol. She talked in a soft voice and seemed very nervous and tentative about taking on any kind of exercise program. "I just want to make sure I don't do

> There is more hunger for love and appreciation in this world than for bread.
>
> Mother Teresa

too much. I don't want to get hurt since I'm not very athletic," she admitted, wincing as she looked at the daunting equipment.

"Don't worry, Kim, we'll start nice and slow so that you are always comfortable. The important thing is to make a start and to start where you can make it, and that is exactly what we'll do. You've already made it successfully through the first step—coming in the door and asking for help. The second step is to trust me and follow my directions because I truly care about your well-being and I won't leave your side. You don't have to go through this alone. I'll be there for you every step." (Not every client gets that much coddling, but I could tell she needed every bit of encouragement I could offer.)

She smiled nervously and nodded her head. Then she looked straight at me and in a much stronger voice confided, "I *hate* exercise."

"You do? Kim, why? Did something happen to embarrass you? Does it hurt? What is going on?"

Her voice still strong, she replied, "I hate it because I hate my father." Then the whole story came spilling out. "My dad was a world-class swimmer but never made it to the Olympics, so he vowed that his children would. So my two sisters and I became swimmers at a very young age. When it became apparent that we were not ever going to be fast enough to reach the Olympics, he switched us to synchronized swimming and pressured us relentlessly. He would say things like, 'You just don't work hard enough. Are you lazy? Yes, you are the laziest girl I've ever known! A pig could swim better than you.'

"At first I tried even harder because I wanted so badly to please him and do my best. But eventually I just stopped trying. When I stopped swimming, he stopped talking to me. He called me my freshman year at college and said, 'Don't come home anymore because you've nowhere to stay. We've converted your room to an office.'

"It was the final blow of rejection. Now all my hurt is turned into resentment. I've never gone near a pool, nor have I taught my children to swim. I've allowed my weight to balloon up because he always told me I was fat. I'm doing it all just to get back at him. The only reason I'm here is that, in spite of all the pain inside of me from twenty-five years ago, I don't want to die."

I felt like a dagger had been plunged into my own heart and was being wrenched with her every sentence. I too had known a childhood without my daddy's acceptance and it was crushing. I sat there stunned as I searched for the words to comfort her. When acceptance is based on conditions—"if you perform," "if you get straight A's," "if you lose weight," "if you go to the Olympics"—children learn that they can never be good enough. Feeling unaccepted by those most important to them is the quickest route to poor self-image and a devastated spirit.

In Kim's case, the lack of acceptance was manifested in those ways as well as her lack of confidence and distaste toward any kind of exercise or care of her body. Who can blame her?

In *How to Be a Hero to Your Kids*, Josh McDowell makes this statement:

> There is nothing more important for a parent to learn and practice than unconditional acceptance. That's why acceptance must come first in building your relationship with your children. The more

you can communicate unconditional acceptance to your children, the more prone they will be to be open, to share and tell you what's happening in their lives.[8]

If we want the communication lines to stay open during those all-important teen years, the younger we start communicating unconditional acceptance to them the better.

Just a month ago, Evan's Little League team was playing in their end-of-the-season tournament. They had lost only once all summer and everyone had high hopes for placing first and taking home the championship banner. The kids played their hearts out and it was looking good. Then the opposing team rallied and went ahead 4-3. But at the bottom of the last inning, Evan's team managed two hits and placed runners on first and second base with two outs. Evan was on deck and Mike was behind the plate umping.

My heart began to pump faster as I saw the pressure mounting for both my son and husband. I began to play out the various scenarios in my head: If the player up to bat got a hit, the bases would be loaded, and it was even possible that the boy on second base could score and tie the game! Or he could get the third out and the game would be over with us losing, which would be OK—just as long as Evan didn't have to be the last out. I knew how embarrassed he would be. Oh, how I wanted to save him that agony!

But it was not meant to be. The player got a walk and Evan was up to bat. The first pitch—*Strike one!* The second pitch—*Strike two!* Evan turned and looked at his dad as if to say, *What are you doing? You're supposed to help me!* The third pitch—it looks good to Evan, so he begins to swing, then realizes it's too low and takes his swing back, hoping his dad would call it a ball—*Strike three! Batter's out! That's the game!*

Whoever coined the phrase "agony of defeat" hit it right on the money. Evan's team was devastated. You know kids are upset when you see tears in public from preadolescents—especially boys. They somehow managed to collect themselves enough to shake hands with the opposing team and then slowly walked to the parking lot with their parents to go home.

As difficult as it was for Mike, I was proud of him for making the right call. He didn't feel pressure to enable Evan to be the hero with a little help from dad. He didn't need Evan to be more than he was, and he wasn't going to help him be something he wasn't. He showed Evan acceptance by making the tough call—and with a trip to Dairy Queen for his favorite Blizzard to celebrate a fun and memorable season.

When we accept our children for who they are, not forcing or enabling them to be what we want, there is always cause for celebration.

Attention

Another emotional need that often goes unnoticed is attention. Are we available to spend time with our children? Do we know what their favorite music group is or their favorite flavor of ice cream? Are we investing in their little hearts so that when they become teenagers and start questioning their worth, they will know beyond a doubt that they are known and loved?

Everyone makes jokes about the hectic pace at which we all seem to be living, but it isn't funny. Parents are busier than ever and where does that leave the kids? Alone?

> Praise is the warmth and tenderness all of us need to change for the better.
>
> *John Drescher*

Josh McDowell writes:

> I'm convinced that one of the biggest myths we have going today is the myth of "quality time." Of course we all want those quality moments with our kids. But you don't get them by appointments or on some kind of tight schedule. You get quality moments by spending larger quantities of time with your children. Out of the quantity comes the quality.[9]

While carpooling is extremely valuable and helpful, when extra kids are around, my kids just don't share their feelings like they do when they are alone with just Mike or me. So we have begun taking one of them with us to run even mundane errands because it's an opportunity to talk about the day or whatever subject comes up. Since we live on the outskirts of town, it's a good fifteen minutes to get anywhere—that gives us at least a half-hour of time together. It has become invaluable time (although not perfect because we still have to concentrate on driving) and has produced some special quality moments.

However, it is possible to give your children your attention without giving them yourself. Last Sunday was one of those summer days you never want to end. It was a crisp 72 degrees, sky as clear as crystal with a slight breeze out of the north. After church, we ate a quick lunch on the patio and headed out to play putt-putt golf.

The course was the busiest I've seen it in quite some time and as we were deciding where to begin, we spotted a dad with his two sons. The only reason we knew he was their dad was because they kept yelling, "Dad, did you see that? I almost got a hole in one! Hey, Dad!" Their dad was walking the holes with them, not playing golf but reading a book. He would occasionally look up, nod and smile at them, then go back to reading. His body was there, but not much more.

Sporting events are another area where you can show up and pretend you are being attentive—you've got your body in the seat and you know the score at half-time—but your kids know the difference between meaningless attention and when you are investing your whole heart.

Evan's soccer games last an hour and are divided into four quarters. Usually each child will sit out one quarter so everyone can play. With this in mind, last year I took one of my favorite magazines with me to read during the breaks. But after the game, when Evan relived every point and play of the match, I felt a little out of touch with the specifics. I had allowed myself to continue reading my magazine past his break and into his playing time, engrossed with an article on excellence in parenting. (How ironic is that?)

"Mom, did you see it when I passed the ball all the way downfield to Jonathan in the third quarter?"

"Uh-huh."

"What did you think of our new offense?"

"Great, looks good."

"I saw you looking down a lot. Were you reading or something?"

Caught like a deer in headlights, I vacillated between throwing the magazine out the window and taking an oath never, ever to read a magazine in his presence again. Instead, I chose the appropriate response, and that was to apologize.

"Evan, I was trying to do two things at once and I ended up missing part of your game. I'm really sorry. Would you forgive me?"

"Yeah, sure, Mom."

I know he forgave me, especially since I haven't done it since, but I also know that he noticed when I wasn't wholeheartedly paying attention. Even on the soccer field in the midst of dribbling, kicking, chasing and tripping, he noticed. It means everything to them.

> It is not a slight thing when they, who are so fresh from God, love us.
>
> *Charles Dickens*

When I was in grade school, my Brownie troop had a parents' night at the YMCA to showcase our projects and paintings. I asked my friend, Sharon, if her folks could give me a ride because mine wouldn't be going. She said yes, so they picked me up and I felt so relieved to have parents—even if they weren't mine—to walk in with. After we picked up our pictures and art projects from our troop leaders, they had all the Brownies sit in a large circle with the parents sitting behind.

Then Mrs. Julian cleared her throat and cheerfully spoke into the microphone. "Parents, I am so proud of these girls. You just wouldn't believe how hard they've worked on these pictures so they would have a gift to give you on this special night. Girls, how about it? Are you ready for your parents to see your projects?"

I felt a knot in my throat.

"Let's take a few minutes so everyone can take their paintings over to their parents!"

No, please, no.

The floor cleared with a flurry of chatter, giggles and squeals, while I sat there alone hoping no one noticed. I wanted to crawl through a hole in the floor, never to show my beet-red embarrassed face again. As the seconds turned into minutes, I glanced at Sharon and her parents, desperately hoping they would pretend to be my family and wave me over. They did, and they were so kind to me the entire night.

When I got home I went straight to the trash can and threw away all my paintings from the evening. My parents never did see them and I wanted no reminder of the pain I had endured while clutching them.

Why didn't my parents go? No reason was ever given; they simply said no. But in my mind the reason was that I wasn't important enough. I truly felt that if they loved me they would have made more of an effort to see what I'd been working on for two months—for them!

Kids know when parents are genuinely attentive. Would yours say you are? How do they know? What good habits have you developed to spend time with them?

Spiritual Needs

At some point, you will inevitably hear these questions from your children: "Who is God?" "Where do people go when they die?" "How do we get to heaven?" "Is Jesus real?"

Will you be prepared to answer your children with truth, giving them a spiritual anchor to hold on to? Or will you skirt around the issue and tell them it's too complicated for them to understand?

Both Mike and I grew up attending church. We went to very different denominations, but the same doctrine was communicated—developing a personal relationship with God; accepting His Son Jesus Christ as Savior and Lord; believing that He saved us from our sins by dying on the cross and being resurrected and that He gives us eternal life. That common heritage has been a light to our paths and has given us a spiritual alliance with which we can comfortably answer our children's questions and pass down the legacy of faith.

We discovered that some of the best ways to meet our children's spiritual needs are not necessarily through teaching them a formal Bible lesson as a pastor does in a sermon, but recognizing teachable moments for applying God's principles, striving to be living examples of Christ as parents (do what I do, as well as what I say), and finding a church that teaches Bible truth. It's almost impossible to meet your children's spiritual needs if you are not regularly attending the *same* church. This brings unity to the family and keeps your children from being confused over doctrinal issues.

It's not that going to church is what saves us or makes us acceptable in God's sight—only grace can do that. It's that church brings a body of believers together to worship God as they learn side by side how to please him and live a life of love.

Mike and I chose Windsor Road Church because it is interdenominational. Its doctrine is biblically based so it doesn't change according to what is politically correct. The children have their own age-appropriate time of worship, apart from the adults.

My fondest memories of church as a child are all during Sunday school, when we would have a Bible story and make a corresponding craft as an object lesson. I was eager to learn about God, and all the stories about Him revealed not only an incredible Creator, but a loving, gentle Father who wanted to be involved in my life. I accepted Him as my Savior when I was only seven, and I knew exactly what I was doing.

It's critical for children to understand God and all the Bible stories from a clear vantage point. The only way to make it crystal clear is to meet them at their level. We made it a point to become involved in the children's programs so we could talk about their lessons at home in a language they understood. This helps tremendously with our communication, and it lets them know that we value their spiritual growth enough to be involved with them.

Teachable moments

We spend most of our summers at the Indian Acres Swim Club. It's wonderful family time as we play Marco Polo, tag, water basketball and dive for rings. But with any sport, there must be rules that make it safer, and swimming is no exception. One of the most common rules is that you should never run on the deck of the pool. It only takes a little water to make the surface slippery enough to fall and scrape a knee—or worse, as Allie found out the hard way.

Five years ago, on one of those ninety-degree, humid Illinois summer days, we were pooling it and having a grand time. Allie was coming back from the snack bar and the bell was about to ring, ending the safety check when children eighteen or younger were not allowed in the water. It was always a race to see who could be the first one back in, so she ran the last twenty feet to the edge of the pool. She slipped on a wet tile and took a nasty tumble that scraped her elbow, drawing blood. I was already out of my chair, heading over to her when she cried out for me. I helped her up, got her to the locker room and gently assured her it would be all right as I washed off her elbow and bandaged it so she couldn't see the blood.

I knew she would be too embarrassed to go back inside the pool right away so we sat out under a large shade tree and I just held her. I didn't scold her or reprimand her. She needed comfort first. Instruction and discipline would follow after her emotions calmed down. As her crying gradually subsided and all the tears were wiped away, I shared with Allie that I had done the exact same thing when I was little, so I knew how painful and humiliating it was. That brought even more comfort to her, and we were able to laugh together about our clumsiness. Her smiles returned.

That's when I brought in the spiritual application. "You know, Allie, just like the pool has regulations to keep you from being hurt, God has some too." Her interest was piqued and she listened intently.

"God wants to protect you from harm, so He has certain commands that He wants you to obey. If you choose not to, there's a

> Funny how many lessons I'd like my family to learn sound like the same thing I'm supposed to learn myself.
>
> Nancy Moser

good chance you could get hurt in your heart as you did with your elbow. For example, God commands us to love our neighbors. He wants you to continue to be kind to Jordan and Teah, because if you break that rule, they might not want to be your friends. Think about how much that would hurt."

Allie nodded with understanding.

"But even if you do sin and break a rule, remember that God will still love you and comfort you, as I did today. Wouldn't it be silly for me to stop loving you because you disobeyed a rule? God will never stop loving you either."

She smiled and seemed relieved.

"That doesn't mean that there won't be consequences for your actions . . . you're grounded for two days!"

She got more out of that thirty-minute lesson on obedience than if I had preached a perfect sermon to her. It was age-appropriate and came at a moment when her heart was soft and teachable.

Lead by example

Last summer I was able to go on a twelve-day missions trip to Russia. As I was packing my two suitcases, Evan wondered why I was taking so many clothes.

"Evan, I'm going to leave my clothes there for the people because they are very poor. I'm trying to squeeze in as many as I can."

He nonchalantly replied, "Oh," and skipped off to play—or so I thought.

Five minutes later, he was back, with his arms full of clothes—his *best* clothes. "Mom, can you take these to a little boy about my size? Do they need shoes too?" Evan was simply following what he saw. Kids do that. They believe if their parents are doing something, it must be good for them too—no matter what it is.

That's why it is so important that as parents we strive to put God first. Jesus said in Mark 12:30-31 that the two greatest commands are, "Love the Lord your God with all your heart and with all your soul and with all your mind and with all your strength" and "Love your neighbor as yourself."

Are we doing that? Are we leading our children to seek God by our example and to love Him with all their hearts? Or are we teaching them that we don't have to go out of our way to love our neighbor because God understands how busy we are? What they "catch" from us will teach them far more than words ever could. And while that is an awesome responsibility, especially considering our ability to err, we must realize that our children don't need perfect parents. They need parents who can lead them to the One who is.

So how are our children faring? In a 1994 survey involving nearly 4,000 youths from thirteen denominations, Josh McDowell Ministries discovered that less than ten percent of young people demonstrate a consistent belief in absolute truth. Forty percent think that no one can prove which religion is absolutely true. One in five thinks Christianity is nothing special—no more correct in its teachings of salvation than any other religion. Nearly half of these young people base their moral choices on feelings and emotions rather than on a clear standard of right and wrong.[10]

We can't afford to leave this important decision to chance. Kurt Bruner, an executive at Focus on the Family, writes:

Take a look at the experiences of many in the baby boom generation. Bored with religion themselves while growing up, many parents chose not to "cram religion down the throats" of their children—opting out of their most important responsibility so that their kids could "decide for themselves when they grow up." Well, we have grown up. And rather than saying, "Thank you," many are asking, "How could you?—How could you give us nothing in which to believe, no compass to guide our steps, no faith to connect our hearts to something bigger than ourselves?"[11]

The bitter aftertaste of being raised without a relationship with God is motivating many parents to give something better to their children. Not that they want to "cram religion down their throats," but neither do they want them to drown in the emptiness of a life without God. Many parents are searching for resources, books, tapes and videos to help in this process, and there are some excellent ones available. Check out *Parents' Guide to the Spiritual Growth of Children* by Dr. John Trent, Kurt Bruner and Rick Osborne; for eight-to-twelve-year-olds, *My Time with God: 150 Ways to Start Your Own Quiet Time;* and *Bedtime Blessings* by Dr. John Trent.

My personal favorite is the series *Family Night Tool Chest*. It's a compilation of books on character, faith, honesty, prayer, etc., that make it fun for kids of all ages. In every lesson there is a family activity that kids can relate to and have fun with which always makes it more memorable.

For example, the topic of "sin" has you take a flashlight and go down in the basement or outside in the evening and capture some bugs in a jar. If you have children who are squeamish around spiders and mealy bugs—all the better. They'll never forget the experience! Then take the jar into the kitchen and set it on the counter so everyone can see the critter struggling to get out.

Here's the moral of the story: "You see, kids, how that bug is trying to escape? No matter how hard it works, it can't save itself. That's what sin does to *us*. We become prisoners of it and we can't get out no matter how hard we try. It can suffocate us so we can't breathe and eventually kills our souls."

Then open the lid and set it free outside. "But Christ came to free us and has saved us from sin by dying for us. He's the only One that can open the jar. Because He died, we can live."

Powerful stuff, yet simple enough for a child to understand. All of these books can be found at www.family.org or at your local Christian bookstores. There are also Bibles available now that are age-appropriate, using words kids understand, and including interesting scientific and archeological discoveries that make the stories come alive.

Conclusion

Children need many things: some needs are basic and simple such as food, sleep and affection. Others take more effort and forethought, as in emotional and spiritual matters. But all contribute to the legacy you will leave them, for the way in which you rise to the occasion and satisfy these deep longings in them will reflect what is important in your own heart.

Discussion Questions

1. What meaningful legacy from your parents or grandparents will you strive to pass on to your own children?
2. What one encouraging word would you use to describe each of your parents? How do you want your children to describe you?

3. Is there an issue of forgiveness that needs attention? What is God's example of how to handle this according to Psalm 103:10-13?
4. In each of the three areas (physical, emotional, spiritual), what new habits are you being nudged in your heart to begin?
5. How can you include those new habits in your daily activities?

Endnotes

1. Josh McDowell, *The Disconnected Generation* (Nashville, TN: Word Publishing, 2000), p. 50.

2. "How Many Zzzz's Do We Really Need?" *Today's Christian Woman*, July/August 2000, p. 10.

3. M.J. Rutter, "Developmental Catch-up, and Deficit, Following Adoption after Severe Global Early Privation," *Child Psychiatry* 39 (1998): 465-476.

4. "Medical News," *Health Magazine,* May 2000, p. 98.

5. McDowell, *Disconnected*, p. 99.

6. Kevin Leman, *Becoming the Parent God Wants You to Be* (Colorado Springs, CO: NavPress, 1998), p. 86.

7. Josh McDowell, *How to Be a Hero to Your Kids* (Dallas: Word Publishing, 1991), p. 115.

8. McDowell, *Hero*, p. 65.

9. Ibid., p. 149.

10. Josh McDowell, *Right from Wrong* (Dallas: Word Publishing, 1994), n.p.

11. Kurt Bruner, as quoted in *Family News from Dr. James Dobson,* August 2000, p. 2.

PART 2

EMOTIONAL

Chapter 4

Stress: Soothing an Overburdened Heart

It was one of those days. You know the kind I mean. You overslept and now you're running late. The night before you stayed up until 1 a.m. trying to "catch up" on all your house projects and responsibilities, then lay in bed until 3 a.m worrying about everything still left undone. With only three hours of sleep, groggy and delusional, you're awakened by a child whispering in your ear, "Mom, where are the five dozen cookies you were supposed to make for our school party today?"

Groan.

OK, maybe every day doesn't start that chaotic, but many do, and I'm ashamed to admit that too often my response is not one of excellence.

The phone rang early one Monday morning and I just knew it was a solicitor. Convinced that my clairvoyant skills had accurately pegged who it was, I answered with an angry, *"Yes?"*

The caller quietly and hesitantly answered, "Oh, I must have the wrong number."

"Who are you looking for and what do you need?" I demanded, still irritated and impatient.

"Well, my name is Bonnie Anderson and I'm calling on behalf of the Michigan Women's conference. We are looking for a speaker for our fall meeting and I was given the name of Laurie Ellsworth as a possible speaker."

Uh-oh. Definitely not a solicitor.

After a bit of hesitation, she continued, "Did I dial the right number? Does she live here?"

Now I don't know if it was the devil or the Holy Spirit, but the only answer that came to me was, "Yes! She does live here . . . just a minute, I'll go get her."

As I recall, I did get that speaking engagement but it was only by the grace of God and certainly not because I was a strong, loving and calm role model.

Stress wreaks havoc on our behavior. It makes us tired, crabby and unapproachable. It throws off our equilibrium and interferes with rational thinking. It can make us lose our tempers over the smallest irritation (like a ringing phone) or reduce us to tears over a sentimental coffee commercial.

People are stressed—like the neurosurgeon who quit medicine to open a bagel shop. People are breaking the speed limit of life—like the man who confessed: "I feel like a minnow in a flash flood."

People are exhausted—like the mother of four from LaGrange, Illinois who said: "I'm so tired, my idea of a vacation is a trip to the dentist. I just can't wait to sit in that chair and relax."[1] Dr. Joel Elkes of the University of Louisville says, "Our mode of life itself, the way we live, is emerging as today's principal cause of illness."[2]

We live in a world that produces stress and in a body that responds to it. Although not all stress is bad—any athlete will tell you how critical it is to a winning performance. At certain times, good stress (also called "eustress," from the Latin *eu*, meaning "good") is positive and helpful. A short surge of adrenaline helps an athlete run faster, have greater strength and concentration and perform better than if there had been no stress.

The problem is that our bodies are best designed to respond to immediate, short-term stress. For example, an exciting baseball game lasts only two or three hours—something the body can easily adapt to. The adrenaline ebbs and flows, allowing the adrenal system time for rejuvenation. If this doesn't happen, even good stress can turn bad. If the stress is constant, long-term and relentless, your body has little time to relax and recover between stress attacks. When this happens we experience distress, where the adrenaline actually begins to harm our bodies.

In his book *The Hidden Link Between Adrenaline and Stress*, Dr. Archibald Hart states:

> Anything—pleasant or unpleasant—that arouses the adrenaline system for too long and mobilizes your body for "fight or flight" predisposes you to stress disease. Your body simply adapts to living in the constant state of emergency—and you feel no discomfort until damaging results occur.[3]

Symptoms of distress or stress overload (remember, the right load of stress is good) occur physically, emotionally and behaviorally, but

> *A fool shows his annoyance at once, but a prudent man overlooks an insult.*
>
> *Proverbs 12:16*

probably the easiest to recognize is the physical damage. It can manifest itself in a myriad of ways, including:

- headaches
- fatigue
- weight fluctuations
- insomnia (trouble getting to sleep or staying asleep)
- muscles aches (especially in the back)
- suppressed immune system (frequent colds or flu)
- digestion irregularities (diarrhea or constipation)
- chest pains (angina)

Drs. Jonathan C. Smith and Jeffrey M. Seidel of Roosevelt University examined the symptoms of more than 1,200 subjects and found that of all these factors, gastric distress was the greatest, being four times more common than the next highest symptom (which was chest pain in the form of disturbed cardio-respiratory activity).[4]

Stress is now considered a major risk factor for heart disease, which kills one out of four of us. Think of it! Picture three of your healthiest friends. If you don't think they are going to die of heart disease, guess who is? According to the American Heart Association, nearly a million Americans die each year from heart attacks, strokes and other illnesses related to the cardio-vascular system. This is more than all the other

> Anxiety does not empty yesterday of its sorrows, but today of its strength.
>
> *Charles H. Spurgeon*

causes of death—including cancer, car accidents and infections put together. While personal training at the Mettler Center, a health club combined with physical therapy, we gave health quizzes to the members each week. Several weeks ago, the question was asked, "How many people die of heart related illnesses each year in America?" Unless they worked in the medical industry and already knew the answer, most members guessed far below the actual number! They all responded with, "It couldn't possibly be that many. That's just unbelievable." Unbelievable, but true.

I assure you, folks who have experienced some kind of health crisis, whether chest pains, a dangerously high cholesterol test, shortness of breath and especially heart attacks, are believers. I've had many clients make drastic lifestyle changes: losing weight, exercising diligently, modifying eating patterns and relaxing more often after a health scare. But not everybody gets a second chance to take better care of himself. For some, death is the first symptom of any kind of problem.

We cannot ignore the fact that our state of mind has a tremendous effect on our physical health. Dr. Redford Williams, a specialist in heart research, states: "If we are to reduce heart disease, experts have to start looking at the psychological realm. Mental worry and prolonged stress may directly precede the onset of heart attack."[5]

While stress may start in our minds and produce pain in our bodies, it also adversely affects the way we act. Behavior symptoms are usually diagnosed by those around us. We may not even be aware we are acting this way, but if we listen to what our families and friends say they've probably noticed we:

- get angry over small issues
- criticize harshly
- are withdrawn and unapproachable

According to the American Heart Association, nearly a million Americans die each year from heart attacks, strokes and other illnesses related to the cardiovascular system.

- are restless
- have nervous habits: nail biting, smoking, drinking
- cry often
- overeat/undereat
- sleep during the day

Can you identify with any of those now? Perhaps you've noticed them in the past during times of high stress. Or could it be that you feel twinges of them every day because life is so overwhelming? When I speak at conferences, overload is a common theme people want to discuss with me. I hear comments like:

- "It's like I have a knot in my throat all the time."
- "I feel so irritable. My family walks on eggshells."
- "My head pounds all day long. The highlight of my day is going to bed."
- "There is so much to do, I'm constantly exhausted."
- "If someone asks me to do one more thing, I'm going to lose it."

Even survival seems hard when we feel all of life bearing down on us, leaving no time for recovery and relief. Sometimes we go through stressful periods such as changing jobs or moving that take care of themselves over time. But much of what Americans stress over are the daily pressures that continually mount. The stress that does us in is the stress of high-energy output and overcommitment. The breakneck speed at which everything must be done doesn't allow time for leisure, fun, relaxation or developing close relationships, and it is taking a toll on our health.

Dr. Richard Swenson states,

> Seeing people in pain is my job. No one likes pain. We all want to get rid of it as soon as possible, in any way possible. But physical pains are usually there for a reason, to tell us something is wrong and needs to be fixed. They help us focus. If you were my patient, you would come to me already focused on your pain. Because 80-90% of most doctor visits are stress-related illnesses, this is what I would tell you: "Your symptoms include different kinds of pain that come from working too hard and relaxing too little (overload). If you adhere to my prescription of slowing down, working less, making time for the things that really matter, your prognosis is decreased pain and increased health. Your therapeutic goal is to enrich your relationships with family and friends, thereby enhancing your own physical health."[6]

How it affects relationships

Mike and I don't argue very often, but a while back during a period of high stress for both of us, we had a doozy. We were in our bedroom "discussing" an issue. The more we tried to resolve it (change the other person's mind), the more heated (louder) the conversation became. I rolled my eyes with every point he tried to make and he turned a deaf ear to mine, no matter how loud I yelled.

Ever the diplomatic one, I decided I'd had enough. I turned on my heel, slammed the bedroom door behind me for emphasis, stomped down every step to the basement and plopped down forcefully into my computer chair to finish writing a magazine article on "The

Blessings of a Godly Marriage." I put my hands on the keyboard to type but knew I wouldn't be able to write a word until I came to peace with my angry feelings. So I looked up at the ceiling and lifting my fist I yelled, "You big jerk!" There, all better.

Controlling anger with forgiveness

We feel angry when someone irritates us, so we stew on it until we're hot under the collar. Somebody hurts us; we let it simmer until we're boiling over. Instead of dealing directly with the source of our stress, we burn with anger. Our bodies are kept in a constant state of readiness to fight because anger raises the level of adrenaline. Our hearts race, everything feels tight, we're ready to explode at the slightest provocation. We overreact to the trivial. Every little thing threatens to set us off.

Anger assaults our relationships. Living with imperfect people always requires patience and understanding, but that is almost impossible to give when we hurt physically and we're spent emotionally. The way we handle stress directly affects the healthy growth of our relationships. When we keep a handle on stress, our relationships can flourish. When stress builds in us, anger results and relationships suffer.

Take a look at the people who internalize their stress. They hold all their feelings inside, suppressing their emotions and denying their feelings. They don't complain or nag or confront. But what they've done is actually made the relationship—and themselves—weaker. This may seem like the easiest way, even the most heroic way, to handle a conflict or problem, but the danger is that it causes the pressure inside to become so great that they eventually blow their lids—or have a heart attack. And that is certainly not heroic.

My father was a classic example of someone who internalized his problems. He seemed to be constantly upset but never discussed what was bothering him. We knew he was angry by watching him. His indignant body language, hostile facial expressions, and when he couldn't hold it in any longer, fits of rage and violence, spoke volumes. His first heart attack came at forty-seven, his third and final at fifty-two. I was only nineteen when he died a week before Christmas.

Then there are those who let everybody know they are hurting because their anger and stress are displaced. People who displace their stress unleash it on innocent people instead of dealing directly with the cause.

John Maxwell said, "Hurting people hurt people." It's not that they necessarily want to inflict pain and anguish on people around them, but they are so overburdened and miserable that it comes across in every conversation and interaction.

When I was a student at the University of Illinois I had a classmate named Amy who was not particularly likable. During group projects she made discouraging remarks and often became rude and offensive with her criticisms.

One day when the instructor asked us to work in groups of two, I knew no one would want to be Amy's partner so I invited her to be mine. (I'd been where she was.) As we worked through the lesson together, she kept checking her watch. "Are you late for another class? Did you miss an appointment?" I asked her.

She took a deep breath. "My parents are going to court at 2 o'clock to finalize their divorce," she whispered, with tears welling up in her eyes. "This is the worst day of my life." And with that her flood of tears could not be contained. Embarrassed by her show of emotion, she quickly gathered up her books and abruptly left the room without another word. As the door closed behind her, we heard her muffled sobs as she ran down the hall. No wonder she inflicted so much anger and suffering onto others—she couldn't bear her own.

> Learning to forgive takes practice.

Such pain we bear in this life! The stress of it seems overwhelming a good part of the time. Yet as hard as we try, we can't get rid of it by holding it inside. Nor can we ease our own pain by hurting others. I recently spoke at a conference that offered over fifty different workshops on everything from self-esteem to financial planning. Out of that vast selection, the most popular workshop was on anger! It's a common problem that can so easily get the best of us, causing us to say and do things we later regret.

God knew we would have trouble with anger. He knew that we would disappoint each other, that we would say insensitive and hurtful things, that we would criticize each other mercilessly then do the very same things ourselves. He knew we would have trouble handling it all. In John 16:33 Jesus said, "In this world you will have trouble."

He didn't say we might, or there's a possibility. He said we *will*. We are all in the same boat because every single one of us at some point feels anger when we deal with people who act like . . . people. Perhaps if we were well-rested, unhurried and protecting our health and priorities, we would be more equipped to handle the inadequacies of others. But we are not, so we don't.

The antidote is forgiveness. The ability to forgive relieves stress and anger. Those who can't forgive are likely to carry the greatest stress. When the mind perceives the need for revenge or defense, it keeps the alarm system at a high state of readiness—adrenaline flows abundantly. I learned a lesson concerning my own anger several years ago. In the same month, I came across several different Scripture verses with the same message: Stop fighting and start loving!

Romans 2:1 says, "You, therefore, have no excuse, you who pass judgment on someone else, for at whatever point you judge the other, you are condemning yourself, because you who pass judgment do the same things." Our mistakes and weaknesses may look or sound a little different from those we criticize, but they are mistakes just the same.

Romans 12:10 says, "Be devoted to one another in brotherly love. Honor one another above yourselves." It's impossible to quarrel with someone when you are thinking of how you can honor him. I love what Stuart Briscoe, pastor of Elmbrook Church in Milwaukee, Wisconsin says, "Under the impact of Christ's love for me, I'm no longer free to look at people from purely a human point of view."

Romans 12:18: "As far as it depends on you, live at peace with everyone." Being peaceful and loving is not contingent on him being the same way.

Ephesians 4:32 tell us: "Be kind and compassionate to one another, forgiving each other, just as in Christ God forgave you." Who can be kind and unforgiving at the same time? We must forgive because we are just as undeserving of it.

"Bear with each other and forgive whatever grievances you may have against one another. Forgive as the Lord forgave you. And over all these virtues put on love, which binds them all together in perfect unity" (Colossians 3:13-14).

These are not only commands, but instructions for how to get along with people. Did you notice the action verbs? "Be kind," "Be devoted," "Bear with each other." And then it says forgive. I believe this is implying that when we act loving, regardless of our emotions, feelings of love will follow. So often we wait for it to be the other way around and we wallow in our anger. I wish I could say people never make me angry or hurt me, but it simply isn't the case. Sometimes the matter must be discussed in specifics (as Rene did with me in Chapter 1), sometimes it can be forgiven without it.

Either way, through these Scriptures I've learned to be kinder to those who offend me, and every time, without fail, I feel more loving, more forgiving, more peaceful toward them afterward.

> Stress can ruin our lives. It can cause physical illness, emotional burnout and relational strain. Unfortunately the way we tend to handle it is with medication to soothe the symptoms. But the pain we experience is an alarm system designed to help us. Just like a bell clanging to warn of a fire, this alarm system plays a very important function—if we pay attention to it. Most of us don't. We reach for the painkiller to silence the bell . . . and don't attend to the fire.[7]

In some cases we need to learn how to recover after fighting daily fires that naturally come with living. In other cases we need to learn to *prevent* them! The best way to keep a fire from starting is to reduce the load of the stress in the first place.

> Even when I have pains, I don't have to be a pain.
>
> *82-year-old*

Head it off at the pass, nip it in the bud, take precautionary actions to protect ourselves from it.

How about you? Are you pulled in so many directions it's hard to know which way is up? Carrying a load that's got you down but can't quite put a name on it? So tired and worn out you want to give up? Have any relationships been damaged by your anger and unwillingness to forgive? Here's a plan that will help you identify the source of your stress and show you how to soothe your overburdened heart.

Reducing the Load

Reducing the load has a three-part strategy:

1. Set priorities.
2. Delegate.
3. Know your personality.

1. Set priorities.

For the longest time, I believed that the root of my stress was having too much to do. But when I took a closer look at why I had too much to do, I discovered the real problem: my priorities were not clearly defined. They were hazy and gray, not black and white. No wonder I couldn't protect them. I didn't know exactly what they were! I had allowed myself to say yes to many things that were not a priority and they began to take the place of what I really wanted to do but couldn't. I was always out of time. I had never sat down and specifically examined every little detail of my life, which explained why I was always drifting toward imbalance.

I'll never forget the day I took back control of my life. It was a crisp fall morning with colorful leaves gently falling on the dew-covered ground—a picture-perfect moment and my favorite time of the year. I took a soft quilt and laid it across my lap as I settled into a cushioned patio chair on our screened-in porch. With my favorite cup of hot apple cider in one hand and a pad of paper and pen in the other, I was ready to do some soul searching (or at least some reorganizing). I started with this simple prayer. *Lord, my life is out of control. I know something is wrong with the way I'm running it because most of the time I feel like it's running me! Help me slow down, Lord. Calm my heart now so I can make whatever changes You want. Amen.*

The first thing that came forcibly to mind was a question: "What are the five most important things in life to you?"

That was easy. Family (hubby first, then kids), health (exercising and eating right), relationship with God (reading my Bible, praying), friends (carving out time to be with them, working on knowing them, understanding their love language), career/ministry (speaking, writing, homemaking).

"Now, put them in order. Prioritize them."

OK, my faith is first. Corrie Ten Boom said, "To be much like God, we must be much with God." If I want to live a life of love and grace, then I must spend time with God, being changed and refined by Him. My best time with the Lord is first thing in the morning. I feel as though I receive my marching orders for the whole day and I am more apt to think holy thoughts as I go about my work. Jesus prayed first thing in the morning, and so did King David. That'll work for me.

Family second. Mike comes first and then the kids. God is honored when our spouses are honored. It takes work to do that and to set aside intentional time to nurture and know our mates.

Fitness third. We can't possibly keep up with the hectic American pace if we don't take care of ourselves. Even Bill Hybels, pastor of Willowcreek Church in Chicago (with 16,000 members), takes an hour every day to work out. He says, "I could easily fill that time with 'urgent needs,' but I've come to realize I can't be at my best unless I'm exercising regularly."[8] The same is true for me (and you).

Friends fourth. Hebrews 10:25 says, "Let us not give up meeting together, as some are in the habit of doing, but let us encourage one another." It's tough to encourage someone if you don't know what's going on in his or her life. My friendships need more than a sixty-second update over the phone to survive and grow.

Career and ministry fifth. I'll limit my speaking to once a month and I'll write when the kids are in school or asleep. My homemaking responsibilities can also be done when they are in school. In the summer, I'll include them in whatever I'm working on.

As I wrote them down on paper, I began to feel lighter. I felt the elephant slipping from my back. "Look at your priorities and decide how much time they need each week—not how much time you think you have to give them, but how much time you need to invest in them to keep them healthy. There's a big difference between the two. Then put that on a clean calendar."

I decided to allow an hour first thing in the morning for reading, praying and spending time with God. (When I started doing devotions ten years ago, fifteen minutes was plenty.) I penciled in one night a week for a date with Mike (Saturday) and one night a week for a family night (pizza out on Friday night). Fitness got an hour, five days

> I've learned that the great challenge of life is to decide what's important and to disregard everything else.
>
> *51-year-old*

a week, and it fits into my schedule best before lunch. Sunday night was set aside to entertain friends (as discussed in Chapter 1) and also one evening through the week to meet with a group of folks from our church for a Bible study.

The priority that got the biggest block of time was my homemaking, writing and speaking. Those responsibilities vary with each day but they do require a good bit of time.

After I finished that exercise and saw how full my schedule was, I was amazed how little time was left. I still had many responsibilities and volunteer obligations yet to be squeezed in. Where would they fit? Hmmm . . . I was beginning to see the problem. I had been "squeezing in" my praying once a week or so, working out sporadically, if at all, cramming in a minute here or a moment there for family time.

No wonder my life had been careening out of control. I had not been a poor time manager but a poor priority manager. That was about to change. I felt a surge of excitement flow through me as I realized my life would never be the same. I had a new mission and that was to devote myself and my time to what mattered most: my priorities.

But what about all the other activities I spend time doing? I wondered.

"Place them on the examining table one by one and decide if they can still be accomplished without compromising time for your priorities." (The voice in my heart was the Holy Spirit. His ideas were so brilliant I knew they weren't coming from me.)

The kids' extracurricular programs were the first to be scrutinized. They could each have one per season but could not be on a traveling team that involved weekend overnight stays (which is all of them). We would stay together as a family and not be overrun or separated on our precious weekends. (This was not a popular decision but we've stuck to it, and it has given us more unity and valuable "face time.")

The next activity to be inspected was my volunteer time. There was little if any time left on my schedule so I decided to resign from two committees after serving the time I had committed to. Neither of those two involved my family and I felt compelled to volunteer where we could be together. I would keep my commitment to work on the prayer team since most of the work could be done at home and it would give me the opportunity to share the importance of prayer with our children. I also would continue to volunteer in their classrooms at school for an hour each week because it would give me a chance to see them and give them a smile. That can't help but send them a strong message about how much I value them.

Now even Mike's volunteer time involves our family. This year Mike is coaching Allie's seventh-grade basketball team. He and Allie have grown even closer through this experience because they spend so much time playing, laughing and learning together. His volunteer work has benefited our family because we all pitch in to help, and that brings unity. Evan is the water boy; I make phone calls and organize the paperwork; and David helps analyze mistakes after the game. (What better job for a teenager?)

What a relief! I had decided what was important, how much time to give it each week and what to cut out. Now this was a plan I could live with. Here's how it looks on paper:

> The reason most major goals are not achieved is that we spend our time doing second things first.
>
> *Robert J. McKain*

	Sun.	Mon.	Tues.	Wed.	Thurs.	Fri.	Sat.
6:00	PRAY AND READ BIBLE						
7:00							
8:00	KIDS TO SCHOOL						Soccer
9:00	Church	WORK					
10:00							
11:00							
12:00	Lunch	WORKOUT/LUNCH					Work on house
1:00							
2:00	Family time	WORK					
3:00							
4:00		Homework/Fix dinner					
5:00	Friends over for dinner	DINNER					Date
6:00							
7:00		KIDS' ACTIVITIES				Pizza out with kids	
8:00					Small group study		
9:00		TUCK KIDS IN BED					
10:00							

Now you try it. Pick your favorite room and pull up a cozy chair. Or drive to a park and enjoy the beauty of nature as you begin to create a plan.

- Prioritize the five most important things in your life.
- Decide how much time should be invested in them each week.
- Place them on a cleared calendar.
- Closely examine all other activities and responsibilities. If they don't fit, get rid of them.

Some of the difficulties you may face with rearranging your schedule and beginning to say no when you've never said it before is that not everyone will accept your "no" with grace. In the book *Boundaries,* Dr. Henry Cloud and Dr. John Townsend address this problem: "People who get angry when others set boundaries have a character problem. They see others as an extension of themselves and they become upset when they don't get their way."[9] And even Christians are capable of laying on the guilt when they feel they need you to help them.

Because I know what my priorities are, I've learned to say "no" when my schedule is already full. When my friend Trish called and asked if I could make a meal for a mom that had just had a new baby, I said "no" without feeling guilty because my daughter had a program that night at school. We were eating out with some friends ahead of time so I knew I wouldn't be cooking and it would be too frantic to try to do both.

But she continued to push, "Well, could you at least pick up some fast food? I'm sure they wouldn't mind that." I thought about it for a second and realized I really couldn't help without compromising some sanity and my own family time. So I said, "No, I can't help this time. I'm sorry." I'm beginning to understand why Dr. Richard Swenson said, "Load is not the problem, but overload is." And while not everyone may embrace or understand that decision, it is the right one.

Dr. James Dobson gave wise instruction when he said, "Resolve to slow your pace, learn to say no gracefully; resist the temptation to chase after more social entanglements, more pleasures, more hobbies (more responsibilities), then hold the line with the tenacity of a tackle for the NFL."

Lastly, try to reduce your work hours wherever possible, while still being able to pay your bills, of course. Money is great, but peace of mind is better. And it's hard to feel any peace when you are constantly in a rat race.

Lily Tomlin said, "You know, the bad thing about the rat race is that even if you win—you're still a rat."

I think there's a lesson for all of us in that, and in this next story as well.

A rich businessman from the North was horrified to find the Southern fisherman lying lazily beside his boat, just staring at the clouds.

"Why aren't you out fishing?" the businessman asked him.

"Because I have caught enough fish for the day," replied the fisherman.

"Well, why don't you catch some more?"

"What would I do with them?"

"You could earn more money, and maybe even be rich like me."

"What would I do then?" asked the fisherman.

"Then you could really enjoy life," said the businessman.

"What do you think I'm doing right now?"

Know what your priorities are—and protect them. Everything you are doing may be good, but we mustn't confuse good and best. Cut it out of your life if it compromises what is most important.

2. Delegate.

After you decide what your priorities are, delegate tasks that can be done by others, allowing you to spend time where your specific touch is needed, such as playing with your children, attending their programs, visiting a sick friend. Never feel guilty about getting help with responsibilities such as housecleaning, grocery shopping, lawn mowing, office work, etc. If you can afford to hire them out—great. If your children are old enough to pitch in—even better. Learn to let go of the small things so that you reserve energy for the important ones.

While growing up, we had the cleanest house on the block. My mother worked tirelessly to cook every meal, keep the laundry and ironing done (for seven people, that was no small task) and keep order in our home at all times. As a mom and wife myself, I admire and appreciate her hard work. But I have no memory of her ever playing with me. I don't remember any times where we sat together and read, colored or even talked. Do your children ask you to play with them? Find a way to delegate less important tasks so you can! It's important for them to have a parent who plays as well as works.

I heard a pastor tell a story of a little boy who began to ask his father how much money he made an hour. The father refused to answer but finally gave in when the boy would not relent. "If you must know, I make $50 an hour. Now please stop bothering me with such silly questions," the father said sharply, and went back to working on his computer. That night after the little boy went to bed, he lay awake until his father came up the stairs. When his father passed his room, exhausted from a hard day's work, the little boy called to him, "Daddy, aren't you going to tuck me in?"

"Son, Daddy is tired tonight. I'll tuck you in tomorrow night."

"Daddy, please, I have something for you and I need to give it to you tonight." Curiosity prevailed and the father plodded into his son's room to say goodnight. When he bent down to kiss his cheek, the little boy pulled out an envelope from under his covers. "Daddy, this is all my birthday money and I want you to have it. It's $50, Daddy! Can I buy an hour of your time so we can play catch tomorrow?"

Our loved ones deserve more of us. Delegating helps make that possible. In Exodus 18, Jethro, Moses' father-in-law, pays him a visit after they cross the Red Sea. Moses is working from sunup to sundown resolving all the disputes of the people. He is doing all the work alone, and is trying to serve over a million people.

Jethro tells him, "What you are doing is not good. You, and all these people who come to you, are going to wear yourselves out. You need to delegate some authority to leaders that you trust and spread the workload out" (see 18:17-23).

Wise words for us to live by also.

3. *Understand personalities.*

What benefit could understanding personalities have in reducing stress? Quite a lot, actually. Understanding your personality and those of other people will allow you to make choices that enhance your health rather than undermine it and to better accept how people are different. Take my friend Wendy. She's an extrovert (popular Sanguine) and loves to be around people. She substitute teaches periodically at the school where her children attend. In the winter when she's apt to get cabin fever, she finds it gives her more energy to substitute at least twice a week.

Even though it takes her away from time at home, she ends up being more productive in the long run because she gets an energy boost from being around people. But it increases her stress if she is alone too much.

The person who is introverted, however, feels drained when she is around people. For her, the opposite is true. Her stress increases when she has to be sociable and it decreases when she is alone.

Are you an introverted business person forced to make conversation all day when what you really want is peace and quiet? Are you an extroverted homemaker desperate for adult interaction in the midst of diapers, baby food and *Sesame Street*?

Do you have a Type-A personality (which has also been described as Type-A coronary disease-prone personality)? People who are Type-A tend to:

- have a high degree of competitiveness
- are easily irritated by delays
- are hard-driving and ambitious
- become easily angered and often have free-floating hostility
- feel guilty when they relax
- finish other people's sentences

People who are Type-A are movers and shakers. They get things done, never waste time and tend to be successful in their careers. The down side is that they may not live very long. Dr. Archibald Hart estimates that fifty to seventy percent of us

> Your capacity to say no determines your ability to say yes to greater things.
>
> *E. Stanley Jones*

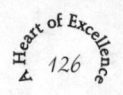

are Type-A, and we are three times more likely to develop heart disease than our Type-B relaxed counterparts![10]

People who are Type-A are not unhappy. They don't mind being hurried. The tighter their schedule, the better driven people feel about themselves and their achievements. They thrive on being faster than others, working longer hours and meeting deadlines. I know this is true because whenever I take a personality assessment, I always test positive for Type-A behavior, and I enjoy my life. That's because the adrenaline rush is seldom unpleasant; it invigorates and excites, but the problem is that it is silently wearing down our bodies. We don't notice it's a problem until it has already done damage.

Chuck Swindoll said, "The only trouble with success is that the formula for achieving it is the same as the formula for a nervous breakdown." The road to success has a price and we may very well pay it with our lives. What I've learned is that even the Type-A person becomes burned out when there is too much to do. This kind of personality has a propensity to suffer from acute stress overload. These folks are going along just fine (or so they think), doing a hundred things at once, and then one day they feel severely depressed, develop an incapacitating migraine or keep waking up in the middle of the night and can't get back to sleep. If you have a tendency to be Type-A, learn to say no and schedule in playtime before your doctor orders it.

Or do you have a laid-back Type-B personality? This kind of personality could teach us all a thing or two about relaxing. When Mike and I were in Kauai, Hawaii (the most remote of all the islands), we noticed a definite change in lifestyle from the mainland. At an outdoor mall, we saw a sign on the door of a shop saying, "Closed, be back later." *As in when later?* We learned by the end of that week that "later" meant . . . whenever. When they were done surfing or napping, when they were finished snorkeling or swimming—you know, whenever they were done relaxing. Life has a slower pace in Kauai, as it does in the heart of a Type-B personality.

While this is extremely advantageous to your health, it may wreak havoc on your ability to stay organized and get to your responsibilities. If you are a Type-B, you should know that your tendency to be disorganized probably causes more stress to the rest of us than to you. Explore your personality so you know what makes you feel more energetic and also more exhausted. Then be proactive about keeping it balanced!

> Prioritize.
> Delegate.
> Understand personalities.

Those are three ways to keep the alarm from sounding. They are imperative to stress management because they hold adrenaline at bay. They are the beginning steps to a more peace-filled life and they are completely under your control. All that's left is learning to deal with what is beyond our control. How do we recover after putting out the inevitable fires? Stay tuned. . . .

Conclusion

Stress is a killer. It can make us sick, damage our hearts and put a wedge between us and our loved ones. When we control our schedules and guard our priorities, our stress cannot help but

> Praise be to the Lord, to God our Savior, who daily bears our burdens.
>
> *Psalm 68:19*

decrease. We begin to feel better because we're taking care of first things first. We'll be making time for what is most important to us, and that wise choice is reflected in healthier relationships and a calmer heart.

Discussion Questions

1. After establishing your priorities, what discoveries have you made about your schedule? What does your new schedule reveal about your direction and goals?
2. Are you a Type-A or a Type-B personality? What habits can you develop to help you overcome your drivenness or lack of discipline? In other words, if Jesus came and stayed with you for a week, what would you change?
3. According to your priorities, what needs to be added to your schedule? Removed or lessened?
4. Read First Corinthians 14:33. How can establishing priorities, delegating appropriate responsibilities and understanding personalities decrease stress in your life and increase order?

Endnotes

1. Richard Swenson, *The Overload Syndrome* (Colorado Springs: NavPress Publishing Group, 1998), p. 11.

2. Joel Elkes, *Time,* June 6, 1983, p. 48.

3. Archibald D. Hart, *The Hidden Link Between Adrenaline and Stress* (Dallas: Word Publishing, 1995), p. 17.

4. Ibid., p. 70.

5. Redford Williams, *The Trusting Heart: Great News About Type-A Behavior* (New York: Random House, 1989), p. 81.

6. Richard Swenson, *Margin* (Colorado Springs: NavPress Publishing Group, 1992), pp. 17-18.

7. Hart, p. 64.

8. Bill Hybels, Leadership Summit speech, 1996.

9. Henry Cloud and John Townsend, *Boundaries* (Grand Rapids, MI: Zondervan, 1992), p. 241.

10. Hart, p. 36.

Chapter 5

Stress II: Persuading Your Heart to Relax

Coping with Stressors

Unfortunately, there will always be stressors in our lives that we cannot control, change or improve. We can't force our boss to be understanding and appreciative. Traffic doesn't lighten up because we're running late. Stretch marks never go away. Our parents will not always be young. Babies cry for no reason. Receding hairlines can't be fixed by even the most talented hairdresser. Death of a loved one always hurts. You can probably think of even more situations you would change so life could be a little easier, but it just doesn't work that way. Some things are beyond our control and they will always cause us stress. We should be prepared to cope with them when they arrive uninvited.

The best ways to cope with stressors beyond our control are to:

1. Be physically prepared.
2. Learn how to relax.

3. Lower expectations.
4. Focus on the big picture.
5. Work it out—with help.

1. Be physically prepared.

Can you imagine what shape our military would be in if the soldiers waited until we were at war to work on their fitness? They don't wait because they need to respond to an emergency with the best that is in them. They exercise daily, limit the amount of junk in their diet and maintain a healthy weight. They are prepared every day to fight for freedom.

We must be prepared for stress as if it were a military attack because it wars against our hearts and bodies. It can destroy our health, our relationships, our communion with God. It can steal our energy, joy and motivation to bring good to others. It is a formidable enemy. Are we ready for its assault?

Before soldiers ever learn military strategy, they get fit. The very first thing they do in boot camp is exercise. Every day they run, climb ropes, do push-ups and sit-ups, scale walls, race through obstacle courses. They push their bodies to make them stronger and healthier. Of course I'm not suggesting we need to scale a wall or climb a rope in the school gym. I am, however, suggesting that we make exercise an important and consistent part of our lives (you'll find fitness help in chapter 8) for three reasons.

First, exercise uses up surplus adrenaline, the main source of bodily pain and disease. Exercise is the one way we can aggressively push stress out of our bodies. Secondly, working out releases endorphins that have a calming effect on our brains. (They keep us from being cranky and losing composure.) Thirdly, exercise gives us energy reserves for those times when we are severely tested (marital strain, loss of a job, financial struggles, etc.).

Neglecting our physical body isn't heroic. It leads to burnout and disease. Only when we exercise consistently can we be adequately prepared for the onslaught of stress.

2. Learn how to relax.

We must force ourselves to slow down. Many of us have been raised to feel guilty about being idle for even a few minutes. We were taught that hard work is good for the soul—and it is. Work was God's idea for us right from the beginning since Adam and Eve worked the ground before sin ever entered the picture. But when we are tempted to think more is more, that's wrong thinking. I believe God rested on the seventh day of creation not because He needed a break, but to give us an example to follow—because we do need to rest. For the sake of our health, we must stop our compulsive activity and force ourselves into occasional inactivity.

Some healthy habits that can stop the flow of adrenaline and help our bodies relax are the following:

Learn to eliminate hurry from your life. Dr. Bernard Gersh, in his book *The Ultimate Guide to Heart Health*, gives these suggestions:

> Making simple changes in your lifestyle can greatly reduce your stress. Try to intentionally drive slower, walk at a more relaxed pace, plan

In the choice between income and leisure, the quest for image has biased us toward income.

Juliet Schor[1]

for appointment delays and traffic jams by having enjoyable reading material on hand. Keep yourself as organized as possible so you're not faced with last-minute rushes to get to your child's game. Put your keys in the same place every time so you eliminate the 10 minutes of frustration when you can't find them.[2]

Learn to laugh. The peak age of laughter is age four. Four- year-olds laugh once every four minutes, or 400 times a day! Adults, on the other hand, laugh fifteen times a day.[3] Humor boosts the brain's natural tranquilizers and releases us from physical and emotional tension. It's hard for the body to maintain a state of anxiety or emergency in the face of laughter. Watch an old comedy on TV and share it with friends. Chances are they could use a good laugh too.

Learn to let go. Jesus didn't heal everybody. Our contemporary drivenness assumes that God never reaches down and says, "Enough, my child. Well done. Now go home and love your family. Encourage your spouse. Rest. Pray. Sleep. Recharge your batteries."[4] I like what family therapist Jean Lush suggests. She instructs people under stress (who isn't?) to give each task on their to-do list a grade. Those that are most important get an A beside them. Those that are fairly important but can be done later in the day or over the next few days get a B. Everything else is a C and can easily be moved to the next week. Let enough be enough.

Learn to stay out of debt. Consumer debt currently stands at $1.4 trillion. Stick to a budget. Pay off debt. Avoid future debt. Eighty-six percent of those Americans who have voluntarily cut back their consumption say they are happier as a result.[5] Many purchases are bought on impulse. If we really need something, let's plan for it.

Learn to schedule time for leisure. Although people will pay to fix their stress, they are not about to change the lifestyle that is causing it, says David C. McCasland. Sometimes we must force ourselves to have fun. It's good for us, for our families, for our health. Educational consultant Buck Sterling says our children will remember two things: "How much love was in the home, and how much time you spent with them." When you spend time laughing and having fun, love is communicated.

Learn to sleep more. The Wall Street mantra is "Lunch is for losers. Sleep is for suckers." On the contrary—to be well-rested is not a waste of time, but a blessing to us and those that have to deal with us. Enjoy a nap without feeling guilty. Sleep is an important antidote for the stress of everyday living, and those who sleep better are less damaged by their stress. The National Commission on Sleep Disorders recommends that the average person gets a minimum of seven to eight hours of sleep.

Sometimes all it takes to brighten our spirits is to take a deep breath in a new environment. Dodie Smith said, "I have found that sitting in a place where you have never sat before can be inspiring." To indulge in a little avenue of escape that changes the scenery—and our attention—can bring us enough pleasure to lighten our load and help us consider our problems

> Let no debt remain outstanding, except the continuing debt to love one another.
>
> *Romans 13:8*

more rationally—or forget them more readily. Sometimes, maybe all we need is that breath.

Use the list below and try to implement at least one of these each week. Or make up your own list of what you find relaxing.

1. Get a massage.
2. Go to a park and read during your lunch hour.
3. Take a class to develop a hobby.
4. Get a manicure or pedicure. (Don't be silly—of course real men get them!)
5. Go for a drive in the country. Pick wildflowers for a centerpiece.
6. Take a walk on a nature trail.
7. Take some friends and hike in the closest national park.
8. Have lunch at a sidewalk café (weather permitting).
9. Curl up with a good book on a cozy sofa at the bookstore.
10. Visit a friend and talk over a light dessert.
11. Hunt for antiques.
12. Go horseback riding.
13. Become a specialist in one small area that interests you. (For me that is travel, gardening and decorating.)

Here are some other gender-specific suggestions for relaxation.

Women
1. Take a bubble bath.
2. Play music and sing/hum.
3. Call a friend who lives out of state.
4. Start a craft.
5. Take a nap.
6. Write in a journal or write a poem.
7. Have a good cry.
8. Have a good scream.
9. Try new painting techniques for decorating.

Men
1. Play your favorite sport.
2. Start a wood project.
3. Check out the biography of your favorite athlete.
4. Attend a sporting event.
5. Take a nap.
6. Organize your garage tools.
7. Check out the newest issue of your favorite health magazine.

Regardless of how you choose to relax, make sure that you keep scheduling it in. It's not a luxury. It really is necessary to play and have fun—or to do nothing but watch the clouds. We wage war against stress when we stay relaxed and calm. We are at its mercy when we only work.

3. Lower your expectations.

A surefire way to increase your stress load is to expect perfection from your spouse, children, job, friends—even yourself. You'll spend a lot of time being disappointed and frustrated that your ideals are not met. What you want is unattainable—at least on this side of heaven. Have friends ever disappointed you and you thought, *If they really cared for me they wouldn't hurt me*? Has your boss failed to acknowledge your hard work or the new account you just acquired and you thought, *Maybe it's time to look elsewhere. . . .* Have you ever said in front of the mirror, *I need plastic surgery to look decent*?

If you answered yes to any of these, you are probably a perfectionist, which means you are causing yourself undue stress. Lighten up.

Perfectionists have very high levels of stress and very low levels of satisfaction with anything. Family therapist and best-selling author Jean Lush states:

Perfectionists are often angry people. They usually carry low-grade irritation inside, because nothing measures up to their impossible expectations. They demand too much of themselves, other people, and even God. It's interesting to me that out of all the personality types, perfectionists have the highest rate of depression.[6]

One of my friends, Sandy, is a marathon runner. Last year she ran the Twin City Marathon in August, then the Chicago Marathon in October. She was so disappointed that her Chicago time was slower than the year before that she battled depression for months.

First of all, most fitness professionals would advise against running two marathons so close together because your body simply doesn't have time to recover. Secondly, less than one percent of the entire population ever attempts a marathon, let alone finishes one. That should have brought Sandy great comfort and even exhilaration over her accomplishment, but because she wanted perfection and wouldn't accept any less, she spent the entire winter agonizing over what she perceived as a subpar performance.

Susan Yates, in her book *And Then I Had Kids*, goes into great detail about the pain of unrealistic expectations when raising children. She reminds us that before we had kids, we vowed to keep them free from even the smallest speck of dirt. We promised they'd never misbehave or

> Good health is true wealth.

embarrass us in public. We were confident they'd get straight A's in school. And then . . . guess what? They don't match up to our expectation, and we feel cheated—or guilty. We must stop this insane notion that life can be perfect—if we try harder, if our mate is more thoughtful, if we lose weight, if our friends reach out more, if . . .

Perfectionism makes us weary, not confident. If we learn to lower our standard for ourselves, our relationships and what it takes to satisfy us, we'll dramatically reduce our stress and notice a marked improvement in our peace of mind.

4. Focus on the big picture.

Along with keeping your body healthy, learning to relax and lowering your expectations, you will take a monster bite out of stress when you focus on the big picture. Helping the less fortunate is one of the best ways to see beyond your own pain. On my missions trip to Russia, I received a big dose of reality right between the eyes. The family that I lived with for a week did not own a car. They walked a half mile for groceries every three days and carried them home.

They wanted more children but could only afford one. Their home had no hot water (they had to boil it) and they worked from sunup to sundown to earn the $75 they lived on each month. Yet they showered me with love and affection and spoke of the joy that Jesus had put in their hearts since accepting Him as their Lord and Savior.

One night, my Russian family asked me (through the interpreter) to show them where I lived on the map. When I pointed to Illinois, they circled it with a pen and told me they would remember me and my family in prayer every time they looked at it.

Then Kolya, the dad, showed me where his twin brother lived, about a two-day journey from them. When tears welled up in his eyes, I asked if he was able to see him very often. He unfolded the whole heartbreaking story of how his parents had split up when he and his brother were babies. He went with his mom because he was sick more often and had a smaller build. His dad took his brother—and they never saw each other again. They learned about each other when they were in their thirties, but weren't able to track each other down, due to the size and politics of the country, until last year—when they turned forty. He could barely contain himself when he announced that they would be seeing each other for the first time in just a few weeks!

By then, I was so beside myself with emotion that it was all I could do to keep my running mascara from staining their sofa. Imagine the pain of those ten years—knowing that he had a twin brother, but not being able to find him, imagining what could have been for the thirty years before!

My Russian family shared many tragic stories, but they always ended them thanking God for bringing them through and that they hadn't suffered worse. That trip and the perspective it gave me made all of my problems seem trivial. If Kolya and his family could be joyful when they had so little except each other and their faith, how could I do any less? Whenever I'm tempted to feel overwhelmed by my problems, I remember my Russian friends. By looking beyond myself and my small world and focusing on the bigger picture—that there are people whose suffering is so much greater than my own—I am reminded to be grateful. I've noticed that the more grateful I am, the less stress I feel.

While we can't all jump on the next plane to Russia, we can get renewed perspective by helping those in need right here at home. I find that visiting the nursing home with my children and holding the hand of the lonely melts my own pain. Delivering food to those who barely have a roof over their heads reminds me that I have so much more than I need. Passing out toys and stuffed animals at the children's hospital ward makes me grateful that my children can be noisy and drag dirt in on their shoes because they're healthy enough to play.

We must allow ourselves to visit the pain of others to keep us from believing the worst in our own. When we help those who are hurting, we receive an extra dose of gratitude in our hearts. Our own worries seem small when we are able to see the big picture. Not that our problems go away—they just no longer have power over us. We trade our stressed-out, angry hearts for hearts filled with godly perspective.

5. Work it out—with help.

Just as we must have the energy reserves to combat stress, we must also learn to confront the root of our stress with tact and love. If we develop spiritual depth by praying and reading the Bible, we'll be able to work maturely through difficult issues. By establishing a closer relationship with the Lord, we can confidently empty our hearts of anger and hostility in exchange for peace and reassurance. Does that mean that once you start reading and praying you'll finally get that job promotion you've been deserving? Does it mean your rocky marriage will tomorrow be delightful? Does it mean that your sick child will instantly be cured or your financial resources abundant? No, it doesn't guarantee any of those.

What it does mean is that Jesus can give us a new perspective and allow us to see with His

> Anxiety is the result when our hopes are centered on anything short of God and His will for us.
>
> *Billy Graham*

eyes. When we learn to obey His Word and listen to His voice, we'll be able to respond to stress and anger in a whole new way.

After my argument with Mike (described in the previous chapter), I sat in my computer chair, fuming. I heard the Voice in my heart say, "What just happened?"

"We had a terrible fight and it was all Mike's fault. Did You hear what he said to me, Lord?"

"Yes . . . I heard. And what did you say to him?" the Voice calmly asked.

"Well, I probably wasn't very nice . . . but he antagonized me. You heard how hurtful he was."

Silence.

"Well, didn't You, Lord?"

More silence.

"What did I do wrong?" I demanded to know.

"Laurie, your obedience to Me cannot be contingent on his. You are responsible for you. Were your words gentle and kind, as Mine are to you? Or were they selfish and impatient? Did you honor Me by honoring him? Were you humble?"

I knew I was hearing the Holy Spirit speak to me because I would never ask myself those questions. I'm too arrogant and prideful. Too bent on being right. Realizing I was fighting a losing battle against Someone who could see my heart, I capitulated. "No, Lord, I wasn't humble. You're right. I shouldn't have said those things and stormed off. I'm sorry," I confessed.

At that point I was really hoping I'd hear, "All right, Laurie. I can see you've learned your lesson. Continue with your writing." Instead, I heard, "Show Me you're truly sorry. Go apologize to Mike."

I groaned. "Isn't there something else I could do? I don't feel like making up yet." I knew the answer. Even though there had been no resolve in the argument and I wasn't sure if Mike would even accept my apology, I trudged back upstairs, opened our bedroom door just enough to stick my head in and say as humbly as possible, "Mike, I'm very sorry I blew up. I said some things I shouldn't have and I'm sorry for hurting you." Giving him no chance to reject my white flag, I quietly closed the door and headed down the steps.

I felt better. I had done the right thing—the obedient thing—and I felt lighter. As I began fixing two cups of hot chocolate (one as a peace offering) in the kitchen, Mike came down and put his arm around my shoulder. "Thank you for your apology. Would you forgive me for being so angry? I'm the one who's sorry." Every bit of hostility melted away as we enjoyed a sweet kiss of restoration.

I'm so thankful the Holy Spirit counseled me against my better judgment or I'd probably still be down in the basement fuming—and sinning. When we see the problem from God's eyes, we see clearly because God's vision is 20-20. When we allow the Great Counselor to change our perspective, regardless of whether our pride agrees, we will protect our relationships and defeat stress every time.

Do you have any relationships that are strained? Would you like some guidance to get along with people better? To have joy and contentment in your life instead of hostility or despair? If so, spend time in the presence of your loving heavenly Father, and He will help you see more clearly. Maybe it's time to soothe your angry heart.

Conclusion

The battle for health begins in our hearts. There will always be certain situations that are beyond our control. If we learn to handle them appropriately, we will preserve our strength. But if we don't take proactive steps to relax in the midst of them, we are headed for disaster. After all, stress is a relentless, inevitable part of living on earth!

What are we doing to physically prepare our hearts for the challenge of living in a harried world, where relationships are broken and the pressure to accumulate is overwhelming? And what are we doing spiritually to keep a proper perspective on what really matters? Spending time in prayer and Scripture meditation keeps us focused on the right things, the most important things—loving people and dispensing grace. Only a relaxed heart can make that happen.

Discussion Questions

1. Rate your physical fitness on a scale of 1 to 10. When, if ever, has it been higher, and what were you doing then? What changes need to take place for it to be rated excellent (8 to 10)?
2. Identify three sources of daily stress that cannot be changed. (For me, it's traffic, phones ringing and answering mail—both e-mail and snail mail.) What techniques can you use to manage them better?
3. Read Romans 14:19. How can we do a better job "keeping peace" in our lives and with those around us? How can we resolve conflict and keep the relationship from falling apart at the same time?
4. Read First Peter 5:6-7. What does it mean to "humble yourselves"? Why does that verse come before verse 7?
5. How does acting on God's Word persuade your heart?

Endnotes

1. Juliet Schor, *The Overworked American* (New York: Basic Books, 1992), p. 123.

2. Bernard J. Gersh, *The Ultimate Guide to Heart Health* (New York: William Morrow and Company, 2000), p. 213.

3. Swenson, *Overload*, p. 80.

4. Ibid., p. 36.

5. John deGraff, producer, *Affluence* (PBS special), aired September 1997.

6. Jean Lush, *Women and Stress* (Grand Rapids, MI: Fleming H. Revell, 1992), p. 39.

Chapter 6

Jealousy: Conquering a Heart That Divides

Throw a little salt in the wound, God. It's bad enough that all the work I've done and money I've spent to produce an exercise video is wasted since it's been rejected by the production company, but now another woman, who isn't even a professional instructor, has been chosen over me. Lord, I know You made the universe, but You're wrong this time.

That's exactly what I thought in 1993 when I saw Cindy's video at our Christian bookstore. I didn't think how wonderful it was that there was finally a Christian exercise video. No, I thought, *That should have been me, Lord!*

I'm ashamed to admit that I'm capable of being so jealous. It didn't make me feel good about myself. I'm sure deep down I knew it was wrong, but I felt so justified. I was the one with a degree in kinesiology, not her. I was the one that had been teaching over ten years at the college level; she was a beginner. I clearly had the needed energy, experience and education to make the video a success. I deserved it. So why didn't I get it?

I got a chance to find out three years ago when I heard Cindy speak in the city where I was attending a writer's conference. She was dynamic, bold and empowered. She spoke for two hours and never used any notes. The audience was as captivated by her instruction and poignant illustrations as I was. She gave thoughtful answers during the question time and was patient when the audience kept her over. It was obvious that she really cared about motivating people to get healthier, to move them closer to the Lord and to strengthen their faith.

As I sat there, I heard that gentle voice of correction, "Do you see the good she is bringing to these people? Do you hear the hope she is planting in their hearts? Don't you agree that she teaches with excellence and authority? Now do you understand why I chose her?"

I took a deep breath and let out a quiet sigh. *Why do I have to be so thickheaded, Lord? She was the* perfect *choice. She's a better speaker and certainly more representative of Your humble character. Forgive me for my foolish jealousy, Lord.*

Foolish jealousy. That's redundant, isn't it? When was jealousy ever wise?

Jealousy literally means "intolerant to rivalry." We feel threatened that someone might take what we feel is rightfully ours. Whether that is attention, conversation, money, promotion, affection, position, admiration, love—or a video contract—our jealousy usually leads to irrational behavior.

In my case with Cindy, thankfully it led only to irrational thinking. I didn't ask the store manager to remove the video. I didn't write her a letter telling her how inadequate she was. I didn't picket outside the bookstore. But I can remember a time when my actions followed a spark of jealousy, and they were just as ridiculous.

Two weeks after our wedding, Mike and I were unpacking some miscellaneous things from his boxes. He had gone in the kitchen to grab us each a Coke . . . when I found it. I was horrified! It was a picture of a beautiful woman in an expensive gold frame. I snatched it forcefully from the box and marched into the kitchen. Being the composed and mature individual I am, I waved it in front of his face and yelled, "So you got rid of all your old girlfriend's pictures, huh? Then how do you explain this?"

I caught him by surprise. He looked baffled, as if someone had planted it or tried to frame him. When he didn't immediately apologize, I cocked my head as if to say, *I'm waiting–'fess up*. Finally he closed his eyes and smiled.

"Laurie, that picture came with the frame. My sister Jane gave me that so I could frame a special picture of us from our honeymoon. I was going to surprise you with it."

"Oh," I quietly replied, too embarrassed to even smile. Fortunately my gracious husband eased the awkward situation and held out his arms to hug me. As he kissed my cheek he whispered in my ear, "There's nobody but you, babe." I cried on his shoulder for a few minutes at how foolish I'd been, but before long we were both laughing at the prospect of telling our grandchildren what our first argument was about.

How Jealousy Impacts Us

Jealousy makes us look and sound ridiculous. Just as I embarrassed myself in front of my new husband, people who yield to jealousy often act irrationally and make fools of themselves. We probably all know women who constantly call their husbands at work to check up on them, or men who accuse their wives of flirting when they speak to any man who they think is better-looking than they are.

> Where you have envy and selfish ambition, there you find disorder and every evil practice.
>
> James 3:16

I'll never forget the newspaper article I read about the mother from Texas whose daughter was trying out for cheerleading. There was one girl more talented than her daughter so the mom hired a hit man to kill that girl's mom, hoping to keep her out of the competition so her daughter could win!

It's bad enough that jealousy makes others wonder if we're crazy, but it can also destroy relationships. My daughter Allie and her friend Allison had been friends since they were four years old. They attended the same schools and were the closest of friends. But then in third grade, there was a change. Allison developed other close friends and Allie didn't like it. Not one to sit back and hold her feelings in (wonder where she gets that?), Allie started saying hurtful things to Allison. The more Allison left her out, the more spiteful Allie's words became.

It escalated into a vicious circle until the breaking point: Allie was the only student in their class not invited to Allison's birthday party. She was devastated. We couldn't get any details from Allie about what might be wrong other than she and Allison had not been getting along lately, and we wondered why Allison's parents would allow such division. The day of the party was hard on us all.

A few weeks later, school ended for summer recess and we began our daily trek to the pool.

When we ran into Allison and her family there, I felt my stomach begin to knot, and I watched to see how Allie would respond. "Mom, did you see Allison?"

"Yes, I did," I said, trying to force a smile. "Why don't you go over and say hi?"

When she hesitated, I pulled out some juice bottles and crackers. Holding them out to Allie, I said, "Why don't you see if Allison would like to have a snack with you?"

Allie slowly took them from my hand and timidly walked over to Allison. They ended up sharing the snack and I noticed them exchanging a few smiles. It took most of the summer for them to be comfortable around each other again. When fall approached, I was apprehensive about them continuing to get along, so the night before school started, I prayed with Allie about their relationship. That's when she finally admitted to me that she had been jealous of Allison's new friends and she had said some very unkind things to hurt her.

"Allie, you have put yourself through all this pain because of jealousy?" I asked with shock and disappointment. Tears quickly filled her eyes as she nodded her head.

Needless to say, that was a painful lesson about the divisiveness of jealousy and how it can so easily separate even the closest of friends. There's a reason jealousy is referred to as "the green-eyed monster." It is a powerful emotion that seeks to control with a vengeance. Even Proverbs 27:4 says, "Anger is cruel and fury overwhelming, but who can stand before jealousy?" Apparently, jealousy can cause more damage than suffering from cruelty or rage. That is an alarming reality.

Do you ever feel the sting of jealousy in your heart? Is there someone you feel threatened by because she takes attention away from you? Is there someone you fear may be more intelligent or business savvy than you? Does he speak more eloquently than you? Do you look for ways to criticize those you view as more attractive?

When jealousy finds a home in any part of our heart, it can quickly become its master. When we compare ourselves to others and we come up short, it causes us to fiercely defend what we are afraid of losing. Jealous thoughts give way to sinful actions. A classic characteristic of jealousy is that it causes us to slander others, taking a small grain of truth and blowing it out of proportion to make them look bad and us look good. Jealousy protects the ego at all costs.

Envy is just as destructive as jealousy. It is akin to jealousy, although different in that the person who envies someone is not afraid of losing what is theirs—they envy what they don't have and want it for themselves.

Bill Hybels shares his own struggle with envy when he was a teenager.

> In high school, I played basketball—not well, mind you, but very enthusiastically. I remember sitting on the bench, consciously wishing that our starting guard would get hurt so I could play. I was so envious of his abilities so that every time I looked at him, one thought went through my mind: "I want your position!"[1]

Chances are that the people we envy or are jealous of don't have it as good as we think. Liz (not her real name) is a friend who is both beautiful and smart. She has a flair for color and antiques and decorated her large custom home with rare art and expensive furniture. She is married to Rich, a handsome man with his own successful engineering company. They have a good marriage with two healthy children and are well-known and respected in the community. Liz is the envy of many women who believe she "has it all."

One day while Liz and I were chatting over lunch, I asked her if there was anything she would change about her life. Her answer amazed me. "Laurie, I would give up everything I have to have a husband who is faithful." With tears flowing freely, she told me how she had learned of her husband's affair. Apparently while dropping off some of Rich's dress pants at the cleaners, a note fell out of his pocket. It was a note from his lover thanking him for their "special, intimate time together."

"Laurie, I know people think my life is so wonderful, but it's not. I just wish they could all see my breaking heart right now and they'd realize how good they have it."

Kent and Barbara Hughes believe that jealousy and envy are a serious problem. They write:

> Jealous and envious hearts are unhappy, for there is a miserable pathology there. The Bible unforgettably commemorates this in the case of the prodigal's older brother. His jealous heart makes it impossible for him to share in his family's joy. In fact, he misses the party of his life! (Luke 15:25-30). Then, unable to share in the things that please his father, he suffers further estrangement. His brother becomes to him "this son of yours." He is out of sync not only with his brother but with his father. He is miserable, and alone.[2]

Bob Russell, pastor of a 10,000-member church in Louisville, Kentucky, says, "When we struggle with jealousy, we must seek to overcome it. Jealousy and envy are horrible emotions that can ruin our happiness and destroy the

> A man's pride brings him low, but a man of lowly spirit gains honor.
>
> *Proverbs 29:23*

health of our hearts emotionally, physically, and spiritually."[3] Proverbs 14:30 says, "A heart at peace gives life to the body, but envy rots the bones."

If you have felt the pangs of jealousy, you know that nothing about it feels good or right or holy. But relief comes when we admit we are struggling with it and take steps to defeat it.

The first step to conquering jealousy is understanding what causes it. Below are some of the most common reasons for our jealousy and envy:

- *Insecurity and low self-esteem.* (We easily feel threatened and doubt our own self-worth.) Because we doubt our attractiveness or worth, we are suspicious of everyone around us. Our confidence is lacking and we feel anxiety in normal situations (like I did over the picture frame).

- *Arrogance* (unrealistic perception of our importance). Arrogance causes us to have a distorted view of our importance and abilities. We think we're the smartest, funniest, prettiest of the bunch (as I imagined with Cindy) even when we're not.

- *Immaturity* (no self-control). Immaturity keeps us from recognizing when we are jealous because we haven't learned to control our thoughts or actions. (We don't have to be young in age to still be immature.)

- *Ingratitude* (bought into "grass is greener" theory). We've chosen to believe the lie that the other person has it better. Our focus is way off. We dwell on what we don't have instead of being thankful for all we do have.

- *Temptation* (clever tool of the enemy). Temptation is probably not a reason we usually give for being jealous, and yet it is an effective tool in getting us to sin (saying unkind things to those we can't control, criticizing those we fear are better than us). It's a form of idolatry and is rooted not in the skin, but in sin. When I allow myself to be jealous, I'm saying I believe my truth more than God's truth. I'm choosing sin over obedience.

The second step is to pursue actions and habits that move us toward emotional health and stability. These habits include learning to:

- Let go of the worry.
- Learn to be content.
- Let the Holy Spirit be in charge.

What we can do

Let go of worry. When we resolve ourselves to the fact that wrong thinking is at the root of our jealousy, we can concentrate on changing our thoughts. Instead of allowing our thoughts to lead us into negative perceptions, we can take charge and lead them in a way that provides greater stability and healthier emotions.

Letting go of the worry is a choice. When we view jealousy as worry, we see it more clearly for what it is. Jealousy is worrying that we're going to lose something or someone. We worry that someone else will get our just due. We worry that we're not as rich, as smart or as talented as the person next to us. We worry that others are comparing us. Maybe the only one doing the comparing is us!

Even if those things are all true, how does worrying about them solve anything? It can't! Therefore, jealousy is powerless and futile thinking that can damage our emotions. When we learn to let go of the worry, we can replace it with positive thoughts that increase our confidence and peace of mind—thoughts like, *If I do my best, then God* will be pleased. I may not have the best body at the pool, but I can feel good that I am working toward my best. My friend plays the piano so beautifully; I appreciate her talent and hope I can learn from her discipline.

You get the point.

Learn to be content. Learning to be content also has incredible value for our emotional strength and is a good defense against jealousy. In First Timothy 6:6, God tells us that learning to be content is great gain and worth pursuing. The difficult thing about contentment is that it doesn't come naturally. We must make a conscious choice to feel that way even when we've been slighted, overlooked or hurt. Again, because our thinking influences our emotions, our emotions influence our actions, our actions our future.

Two young gentlemen chose contentment over jealousy, even though they sat at the end of the bench for the Stanford football team and rarely received any play. Instead, they used their bench time to establish a friendship, sharing their goals and dreams for their future. After the men graduated, they remained friends and started a business venture together that became quite successful. They named their company after their last names. Perhaps you've heard of them—Hewlett and Packard. Imagine their loss if they had used their time on the bench to feel inadequate and jealous. It's a loss that would affect the world!

> For the LORD will be your confidence.
>
> *Proverbs 3:26*

Jealousy: Conquering a Heart That Divides

With regard to discontent with your marriage, Rick Warren says, "The grass isn't greener on the other side. That's ridiculous. The grass is greener where it is watered." Every relationship looks better from a distance. It's impossible to see any flaws. But if we devote ourselves to nurturing and caring for our own loved ones, appreciating what we've been given instead of what's wrong, we will begin to see the emerald green on our own side.

Let the Holy Spirit be in charge. Finally, the most powerful way to fight jealousy is to listen to the Holy Spirit. The Holy Spirit is the voice of God inside believers. It is the gift He left us after Jesus was crucified and raised so that we could live empowered lives of love and self-control. God doesn't want our emotions to defeat us through envy and jealousy. He wants to be Lord of our thoughts so that we can receive His peace and contentment.

The Holy Spirit reveals through the Scriptures that jealousy is not God's best for us. Galatians 5:26 commands us not to be conceited or envious of each other. In regard to arrogance, God says, in 6:3: "If anyone thinks he is something when he is nothing, he deceives himself" [or herself, as in my case]. And First Corinthians 3:3 indicates that where there is jealousy, there is sin.

The Holy Spirit also reveals truth through that still, small voice inside of us. That same Voice that spoke to me during my argument with Mike also tried to tell me not to overreact when I discovered the now infamous gold picture frame. The Holy Spirit prodded me to inquire about it, but I followed the leading of jealousy and accused instead. Do you ever hear a gentle Voice encouraging you to speak love instead of harsh accusations?

It is only through the Holy Spirit that Mike and I have worked through this issue, because early in our relationship, jealousy had a tight grip on our emotions. Now, fifteen years later, when we begin to feel the slightest inkling of it, we tell each other and pray about it together. There is incredible freedom in that, but it didn't happen overnight.

As for Allie and Allison, now in junior high, they are great friends again—completely healed and closer than ever. In fact, Mike and I have become close friends with Allison's parents. Recently Allison's mom sent me a card thanking me for helping during their move and for being "such a good friend." Just thinking about that note brings tears to my eyes because I see the beauty of a healed relationship. Where jealousy had tried to divide, God had saved.

With the Holy Spirit in charge of my emotions, my character is becoming more humble and my actions more grace-filled, which is what led me to speak with Cindy after her speech. In the midst of several people waiting to get her autograph, I admitted the jealousy I'd been harboring against her and how wrong I had been. I felt so ashamed I could barely get the rest of my words out to say I was sorry. Not that my jealousy had hurt our relationship because we didn't have one. She didn't know me from Adam and would have never known what grievances I had against her. But I knew—and my heart needed to be free. I left Cindy with encouraging words that affirmed her abilities.

If you feel compelled to ask someone forgiveness, make sure your motive is completely pure. It should reflect humility and should *not* leave the person feeling dumped on. He or she should walk away feeling lighter too. If that cannot be the outcome, then keep your remorse to yourself.

Do you have a heart that longs to be free from insecurity and the sin of jealousy? Is there someone you have treated unfairly? Criticized unjustly? Compared yourself to? Do you envy the good that others have? Are you devoting yourself wholeheartedly to watering your side of the fence?

If your heart is heavy from envy and jealousy, take a moment and ask God to forgive you. Then wait for His voice of mercy to comfort you with love, affection and miraculous restoration.

Conclusion

The battle for our emotions is fierce indeed. Whether we feel overwhelmed by stress and anger or incapacitated by jealousy and envy, our emotions can weigh heavily on us. But there is hope for our hurting hearts that brings relief and freedom. Our emotions don't have to spiral out of control. We can take charge of them by using the principles that are based on God's Word and the lessons learned from trying to live without them. When we learn how to depend on these truths, we'll become strong enough to live victoriously in a world that is not our home, and our emotions will become one of our greatest allies.

Discussion Questions

1. Identify a situation in your life where you've struggled with jealousy or envy. Of the four causes, which was responsible for your reaction?
2. Proverbs 27:4 indicates the power of jealousy. Why is it so destructive?
3. Is there discontent in any of your relationships that tempts you to envy the "grass on the other side?"

> He is the happiest, be he king or peasant, who finds peace in his home.
>
> *Johann Wolfgang von Goethe*

4. What is God's plan for helping us conquer jealousy and envy? How can we develop better habits for being grateful?

Endnotes

1. Bill Hybels, *Laws That Liberate* (Wheaton, IL: Victor Books, 1985), p. 127.

2. Kent and Barbara Hughes, *Liberating Ministry from the Success Syndrome* (Wheaton, IL: Tyndale House Publishers, Inc., 1987), p. 101.

3. Bob Russell, *Making Things Happen* (Cincinnati, OH: Standard Publishing, 1985), p. 117.

PART 3

PHYSICAL

Chapter 7

Nutrition: A Heart Full of Energy

"If I had known I was going to live so long, I would've taken better care of myself," quipped George Burns at his eighty-fifth birthday party.

People are living longer than they used to, which is why it's so important that we develop not only healthy habits for relationships and emotions, but also habits that give us maximal physical health. There are proven ways to have abundant energy and strength. Certain actions bring wellness to our bodies. We can develop these habits and choose healthy actions so each day can be lived with vim and vigor!

Years ago when I started teaching health and fitness at the college level, the same four principles for health and fitness kept surfacing. I wanted to give my students an easy way to remember them so I used a letter from each rule and made the acronym WELL. Now it's simple to remember: "If you want to be well, then you have to live WELL."

It isn't new information. We've all heard these same four guidelines many times. But even though they may be familiar, it makes a difference if we understand why they have such a powerful impact on our lives. When we understand why and how this principle works, we will be more apt to put it into practice and live in wellness.

The four guidelines are:

> W ater
> E at by the food pyramid
> L ift your heart rate
> L ift weights

See? It's not complicated or new information by any stretch. So why use old information when we don't seem to be getting any healthier or fitter? Because it's not the principles that are ineffective, it's the application—or the lack of.

In chapter 7, I'll be explaining the "W" and the "E" part of the WELL Principle, as well as giving quick and tasty recipes that are heart smart. Chapter 8 will cover the "L"s.

The WELL Principle was what saved me seventeen years ago (even though I hadn't given it a name yet) when I gained thirty-five pounds during my divorce. I went from a size five to a fifteen in just nine months. Desperate to lose the weight and claim my health and energy back, I tried every quick-fix weight-loss scheme there was. Nothing worked, until I drank more water, developed a plan for eating right, worked out aerobically five times a week and lifted weights. That was the beginning of health for me. My energy returned, I lost all the weight (the right way) and have kept it off, and feel better than I did twenty years ago.

Trust me when I say diet gimmicks don't work. I tested them all (at least twenty different diets) and while I may have lost a little here and there, it was impossible to maintain such extreme programs. Someone once said, "Learn from the mistakes of others. You can't live long enough to make them all yourself." There is a better way, a more natural way of eating that is not based on deprivation. The path to health is based on normal eating and drinking and its destination is abundant energy and living free of disease. You are about to embark on that journey.

Water

It's true what we've heard: our bodies work best when they have at least eight cups of water with eight ounces in each cup. I realize that is a lot to drink in one day. One of the reasons it's difficult is because we rarely do it, so it doesn't come naturally. It's not a habit. Almost every client I've personally trained initially estimated that they drank enough water. But when I had them actually keep track and count each glass, they were surprised to find that they only drank about half of what they needed.

Try testing yourself. Estimate how many glasses of water you think you drink through the day, then actually count them. Yes, I'm aware that you could skew the test by actually drinking eight glasses! But you would know whether that was normal for you or if you were just forcing it to look good.

Why we need it

Americans love to drink everything but water—soda, fruit drinks, coffee, tea, alcohol. We guzzle 50 million cans of Coke and 200 million cups of coffee daily![1] How can plain water possibly compete? Yet our bodies are made up of two-thirds water. That's ten to twelve gallons! We need such an incredible amount because it is the main ingredient in all body fluids from digestive juices to blood, sweat and tears. It can literally be found in every part of our bodies. That's why we feel more energetic when we get enough of it.

Some of the benefits of water are:

> Eat to live, and do not live to eat.
>
> *Ben Franklin*

- It helps get rid of body waste. Water is the vehicle digestion uses to flush waste from our bodies. It is a natural laxative.
- It is essential for maintaining proper muscle tone since eighty percent of our muscle mass is water.
- It keeps the kidneys and urinary tract functioning properly.
- It helps prevent water retention. Water is a natural diuretic and is the best way to keep body fluids regulated.
- It helps prevent colon cancer by quickening the digestive flow.
- It helps regulate body temperature.[2]

Since we are constantly using water, we are constantly losing it too. We lose it in obvious ways like sweat, urine and tears. But we also lose it in ways that are harder to measure such as through digestion and water vapor when we breathe.

So what happens if we don't get enough? Won't we know if we are dehydrated? Won't we feel thirsty? Most people wait until they are thirsty before they consider taking a drink. In fact, God designed the thirst mechanism as a kind of circuit breaker to tell us we are already at a significant deficit. We need to drink plenty of water *before* we are actually thirsty.

What happens if we're low

Make it your goal never to be thirsty and you won't ever have to be bothered with the side effects of being dehydrated. Usually the first symptom of being low on water is *fatigue*. Not drinking enough water can actually make us tired! It makes sense when we think about it. If every cell in our body requires water to function properly, then how can it do that if we're not drinking enough? Answer: It can't. The result is fatigue. Next time you get an afternoon lull or feel lethargic, check your water intake. If you are low, belly up to the faucet and drink up!

Even the Bible confirms that not drinking enough water will make you tired. You'll find it in Isaiah 44:12. Check it out.

Because our bodies were designed so magnificently by our Creator, they have built-in mechanisms to help us survive when we neglect them. For instance, when we don't drink enough water, our hypothalamus, which is a brain center that regulates our appetite, raises its thermostat and we become hungry. Our bodies get a certain amount of water from food so it saves itself by making us eat more than we may need calorie-wise. Our bodies will not go without water, and if they have to get it from extra food, they will.

Other symptoms include dry skin, dry mouth and poor digestion in the form of irregularity or hemorrhoids.

Not fun stuff, is it? I don't know about you, but I would rather force down some extra water than have to deal with all the dehydration problems.

When I speak at conferences, someone inevitably says, "I know I'm not going to drink that much water. That's just unrealistic for me. What's the bare minimum I can get by on?" That depends on how many side effects you want to put up with. If you don't want any, then sixty-four ounces a day is still the answer.

How to get enough

Most of my clients that become successful water drinkers do so by establishing three habits.

1. They have a special cup or water bottle they always use.
2. They keep it with them as often as possible, like when they are in the car or working out.
3. They keep track of how many times they fill it. For example, if they use a water bottle that holds sixteen ounces, they know they have to fill it four times.

It seems that all three habits must be used every day to really be successful with this.

After all these years I still find those habits are helpful for me too. Let's face it: life requires us to think about 10,000 other things through the day. Water usually isn't at the top of the list of things to get done. To make it less of a hassle, I leave a large drinking cup next to my bathroom sink. Whenever I'm in there, I fill it to the brim and chug it down.

I also limit the amount of caffeine I have through the day because it's a diuretic, meaning it makes us lose water almost faster than we can bring it in. It can quickly dehydrate us, forcing our bodies to retain water—and that's always fun.

Caffeine is also addictive. Manufacturers of soda want it that way. Researchers at John Hopkins University School of medicine concluded that caffeine is actually added to soda, not for the taste, but for its addictive properties. Few people can taste the difference caffeine makes. But caffeine is an addictive and mood-altering drug which surely accounts for the fact that people drink far more sodas with caffeine than without. Approximately seventy percent of soft drinks contain caffeine, and an average of 585 cans of soda is consumed per person per year. More soft drinks are consumed than water.[3]

A quick way to measure whether you have an adequate supply of water coming in is to check the color of your urine. It should be so light that it's almost indistinguishable. That lets you know your water supply is adequately diluting the impurities in your kidneys and bladder.

It is important to note that after a period of profuse sweating, more than an hour of uninterrupted athletic competition or recreation, a sports drink such as Gatorade can put electrolytes back in balance. Electrolytes are calcium, potassium and sodium. These are lost through sweat. (Ever notice how salty sweat is? That's the sodium.) It should be taken within the first hour of rest if possible. Don't overdo it, though.

Water is a key ingredient to our health. We all know we should be drinking it; now we know why. Dehydration has consequences that are extremely unpleasant and they will hopefully serve as adequate motivation to keep us guzzling.

Eat by the Food Pyramid

Food has gotten a bad rap. We hold it responsible for our weight increase. The incidence of obesity in America has more than doubled during the past century, regardless of the fact that Americans now consume about ten percent fewer calories than they did at the turn of the century. Despite our nation's intense preoccu-

> Discipline is doing what doesn't come naturally.

pation with weight and dieting, the percentage of overweight individuals increased from twenty-five percent to thirty-three percent between 1976 and 1991![4]

I'll be the first to admit that food is enjoyable. Everything from the way it smells to the way it fills our tummies is pleasant. Yet so many people deprive themselves of eating normally because as hard as they try, they find themselves getting fatter and fatter. Then they feel compelled to diet but that doesn't keep the weight off for long. Even after working so hard to lose twenty pounds, maintaining the diet that brought them success is another story.

Constant dieting lowers our quality of life and is oppressive to our spirits. Dieting helps us gain weight because it lowers our metabolism.

Actress Totie Fields reinforced that when she said, "I have been on a diet for two weeks and all I have lost is two weeks." (Been there.)

There's an easier way to get healthy. We need to learn how to eat, not how to diet. By using the food pyramid as our guide, we can establish better eating habits that are "user friendly." They're easy to implement and great for the entire family, as well as those wanting to lose weight. It's the way we should be eating all the time. And once we develop better eating habits, our energy will be overflowing and so will our happy hearts.

Because there are so many good books on nutrition from authors like Pam Smith and Nancy Clarke, I will not attempt to duplicate what they have already so effectively written. My goal is to remind us of the basics and why they work and to offer simple and practical suggestions and recipes.

The serving size

We've probably all seen the food pyramid on the back of a cereal box or on the side of a loaf of bread. It tells us what foods we should have and what quantities of each. The bottom of the pyramid is where most of our food should come from: carbohydrates. In spite of the outrageous claims you've heard, carbohydrates do *not* make us fat!

Eating more than we move is what makes us fat. Carbohydrates are 100 percent energy because they are easily broken down in our digestive tracts to a form of sugar called glucose. They are the fuel our bodies reach for first. They are stored in the muscles (in the form of glycogen) for quick release. If we don't eat enough of them, our body will break down its own muscle and convert it to glucose to use as fuel. That results in a lower metabolism, meaning we don't need as much food through the day. What a double whammie!

Carbohydrates are good for us, and anyone who tells you otherwise needs to take a class in biochemistry. The Food Pyramid Plan is embraced by the most credible fitness experts and organizations in the world such as Kenneth Cooper at the Center for Aerobics Research in Dallas, American Council on Fitness in San Diego, American College of Sports Medicine, and Pamela Smith, world-renowned author, registered dietitian and consultant to NBA teams.

Carbohydrates come from plants. They are the only source of fiber (which is another important reason to eat them) and they are low in calories. Complex carbs are found in breads, rice, cereal, pasta, oatmeal and barley (whole wheat is preferable). We need six to eleven servings each day. A serving size is one slice or one cup.

The next two most abundant groups are fruits and vegetables. We should have three to five servings of vegetables and two to four of fruit. A serving refers to a medium-sized apple or 3/4 cup of juice. A veggie serving would be a ½ cup raw or cooked, or one cup raw leafy. Keep the skin on whenever possible for extra fiber.

The meat and dairy group each require two to three servings. For meat, that serving size would be about the same as a deck of cards, which is usually about half the size a restaurant serves. Leaner portions of red meat have the word "loin," and fattier pieces have the word "rib," so choose wisely. Red meat is the most abundant source of iron, so at our house, we cook with it once or twice a week. We also use a lot of chicken, opting for the boneless, skinless kind which helps save time and fat. (The skin is loaded with saturated fat.)

Protein is the body's major building material. The brain, muscles, skin, hair and connective tissue are all composed of protein. Protein works to replace worn out cells and to regulate body functions. Protein is so important we cannot be healthy without it. It's powerful, so we don't need very much of it. Six and a half ounces provides all the protein we need in an entire day. The typical American diet provides us with two to three times the recommended amount. While carbohydrates burn, protein builds.[5]

One cup of milk or yogurt or 1.5 ounces of cheese equal one serving of dairy. I always have a cup of skim milk on my cereal (I don't measure it but you can if you want to know exactly how much you're getting), yogurt for lunch or snack, and milk, either with dinner or in hot chocolate later. It's really not that hard to include dairy products in your eating patterns, but if you find that you are lactose intolerant or just don't care for the taste, you should ask your doctor or a registered dietitian about taking a calcium supplement. Most of us need about 1,200 mg of calcium every day. A cup of milk provides 300 mg, frozen yogurt has almost the same, but no other

> There are no bad foods— only wrong amounts.

food is even close after that. Some juices are now fortified with calcium and that is an easy and effective way to get it. But milk is better.

Since the release of the book some ten years ago that made erroneous claims against cow's milk, many people have an aversion to it. So I looked to the most credible source I knew for the answer—the Bible. I found the consumption of milk sprinkled throughout it, but most convincingly in Isaiah 7:21-22.

Sugar and fats are at the very top of the pyramid and should be used sparingly. Fat is an essential nutrient needed in very limited amounts for lubrication for your body, transporting vitamins and protecting vital organs. But not all fat is good for us.

Saturated fat is the most dangerous form of fat because it raises bad cholesterol (LDL). It is found in all animal fats, butter, bacon, sausage, hot dogs, marbling in meat, as well as coconut.

Monounsaturated fat raises the level of good cholesterol in your blood (HDL) and is found in olive, canola and peanut oil. It helps to lower the risk of heart disease.

Polyunsaturated fat is middle ground. It raises both good and bad cholesterol. It is found in all other vegetable oils such as safflower, corn, sesame, sunflower and cottonseed. It also includes almonds, pecans, walnuts and avocados.

The percentages look like this:

> 55-60 percent of calories should come from carbohydrates
> 30 percent from fat
> 10-15 percent from protein.[6]

When we make a conscious effort to limit saturated fats and increase our complex carbohydrates, everything in our body will become healthier, especially our arteries and digestive tract.

I have to be honest and say that while we have developed some excellent eating habits at our home, we don't always eat perfectly. Evan reminded me of this some time ago when we were discussing how he could make better choices. He asked me if gummy worms were a fruit or a meat.

Why food gives us energy

Does that sound like a lot of food? Are you afraid you'll gain weight if you eat according to the Food Pyramid? We needn't be afraid of eating. Food gives us energy because that is what a calorie is, a unit of heat and energy. The problem with our eating habits is that we tend to eat the opposite of the way we are supposed to. In America, our eating patterns tend to be very high in fats and sugars, with double the amount of protein, a few fruits and vegetables and hardly any bread or grains. That is backward, or actually, upside down.

Grains, fruits and vegetables are the lowest in calorie, providing four calories per gram of carbohydrate. We can get away with eating so much of them because they tend to be lower in calories than fats, which have a whopping nine calories per gram.

Do you see how eating opposite of the food pyramid will cause you to consume a lot of extra calories? You'll consume more "energy" than you use up; you'll have a difficult time maintaining your weight and a near impossible time trying to lose body fat. When we eat correctly, we can take in more food because it has less energy (calories).

Because grains and carbohydrates in general have fewer calories (heat units), we'll need to eat more often to keep a steady supply of fuel coming in. That keeps our metabolism higher and our mood stable because we don't allow ourselves to starve. Imagine it this way: do you keep a room warmer if you build a huge fire and let it burn out, not adding any other wood, or do you keep a room warmer if you are constantly stoking the fire? Of course you keep the room warmer if you constantly stoke the fire. Our bodies work the same way. When we eat four to six smaller meals throughout the day our energy will stay strong and level. The rule is eat wiser and more often.

Most overweight people break these rules and do at least one, if not all, of the following:

- skip breakfast
- eat little or nothing for lunch
- eat eighty percent of their calories in the evening
- eat foods high in fat
- eat large portion sizes

I would add that people who maintain a healthy weight and are successful at losing body fat do the opposite. They run toward health when they fuel their bodies all through the day, starting with breakfast, and keep stoking it with food from the bottom of the pyramid, not the top.

Are you starting to see any habits you could change? Do you keep trying to lose weight but it keeps finding you? Are you ready to enjoy eating again? Begin to make these changes in your eating habits and you will make a world of difference in the way you look and feel. You can be healthy without being miserable. I'm living proof.

Proper eating habits don't come naturally—at least for me. I would much rather munch on a candy bar than a carrot, so I've learned not to make junk food so accessible. Not that we can't indulge once in a while—there's nothing wrong

> *Don't window-shop at the bakery.*
>
> *Carol Weston*

with that. But I'm not like my friend, Julie. She can have a two-pound bag of M&M's up in her cabinet and just eat a few from it every day. That's not my style! I'm an all-or-nothing kind of woman. So I've learned to always keep healthy snacks available that taste great and are nutritiously filling. Here are some healthy snack ideas that give you the best of both worlds:

- pretzels with raisins and almonds sprinkled in
- yogurt to dip a banana or apple slices in
- nutty granola bars (be choosy about fat content)
- carrots or broccoli and low-fat dip
- bagel with fat-free or low-fat cream cheese
- "ants on a log" (celery with peanut butter and raisins on top)
- graham crackers dipped in skim milk
- apple slices dipped in peanut butter
- wheat thins with a thin slice of cheese
- bowl of cereal and milk

Did you notice what these snacks have in common? They all combine carbohydrates with a protein. The benefit is that it keeps your blood sugar more stable, so you don't have a surge of energy and then crash. It will tide your hunger better until your next meal because protein is digested mostly in the stomach. It leaves you feeling fuller than a carbohydrate that quickly moves through the stomach and gets digested in the small intestines. When we combine these two, we do indeed get the best of both worlds.

When I pack lunches for the kids, I always include protein and carbohydrates together. And I make sure to send a drink that is 100 percent juice to limit the sugar that can make them restless in the afternoon and crabby by dinner. (Sending a note of encouragement each day in their lunch box will also benefit their mood!)

While it takes some planning, we can establish better eating habits that leave our fuel tank full and our fat cells empty. We can make a noticeable difference in our energy level by taking small steps toward better nutrition! Careful and intentional planning is essential if we are to build habits that make us stronger.

Meal planning and recipes

One of the most helpful habits I've established is making a monthly menu. It takes about two minutes to make a calendar on the computer. I add a little color, a few graphics symbolic of the month and voilà! I've taken the first huge step toward better nutrition for me and the entire family. Then I sit down with a cookbook whose recipes are tasty, nutritious and can be made in twenty minutes or less. After I've collected a few months' worth of menus, I use them to plan the months thereafter. It's so easy!

Dinnertime has been referred to as the "arsenic hour" but it needn't be so stressful or chaotic. By planning your meals in advance, you can be prepared ahead of time and more relaxed when everyone is clamoring, "What's for dinner?" In the morning, you already know what meal is scheduled so you can set the meat out or put it in a crock pot. If you are missing an ingredient, you can stop at the store on the way home or on your lunch hour. You'll be calmer and your family will eat better when you plan ahead.

I've provided a week's worth of menus and recipes that fall under my prerequisites: tasty, nutritious and can be made in twenty minutes or less. You saw my schedule back in chapter 4, so you already know I'm busy. If I can make these meals, I guarantee you can too! (Remember to share a meal or two with friends and family each week.)

Sunday
Plantation Casserole
Hearty wheat bread (store bought is OK)
Triple Threat Chocolate Cake

Monday
Crudités (veggies and dip)
Glazed chicken breasts
Baked potatoes
Bread or rolls
Orange sherbet

Tuesday
Corn lasagna
Cashew lettuce salad
Garlic bread
Frozen yogurt

Wednesday
Cheesy Tuna (or Chicken) Bake
Your choice of bread
Strawberry parfaits

Thursday
Stromboli
Fresh pineapple

Friday
The one thing I always make for dinner on Friday is reservations. (We usually have pizza out as a family.)

Saturday
Chicken breasts on the grill
Lettuce salad
Baked potatoes
Whole wheat rolls
Orange Jell-O salad

Recipes for Sunday

Plantation Casserole
1 lb. lean ground beef
small bag frozen corn
3/4 c. skim milk
8 oz. noodles, cooked
1 can cream of mushroom soup
1 8-oz. block of fat-free cream cheese

Brown meat in large skillet. Stir in milk, soup and cheese until well-blended. Add corn and cooked noodles, heat through. Salt and pepper to taste.

Triple Threat Chocolate Cake
Sweet Rewards sour cream chocolate cake mix
1 sm. package choc. instant pudding
½ c. water
4 eggs
1 c. fat-free sour cream
½ c. applesauce (without cinnamon)
1 tsp. vanilla
small bag of chocolate chips

Combine all ingredients, except chocolate chips, and mix in large bowl. Beat for 4 minutes. Stir in chocolate chips. Pour into greased and floured bundt pan. Bake at 350 degrees for 50 - 60 minutes. Garnish with strawberries and powdered sugar.

Recipes for Monday

Crudités
Use your favorite veggies and healthy ranch dip

Ranch dip
2 c. nonfat plain yogurt
1 pkg. ranch-style salad dressing mix

Stir together and refrigerate for an hour. Serve with veggies.

Glazed chicken
Spray the bottom of a 9 x 12 pan. Place frozen chicken breasts in pan. In medium bowl mix 2 c. ketchup, 1/4 c. lemon juice, 1 c. brown sugar and a dash of Worcestershire sauce. Pour over chicken and leave uncovered. Bake at 350 for 1½ hours.

Baked potatoes
Wash 6 potatoes (or however many are in your family) and cover with foil. Place in oven with chicken and let bake same amount of

time. Garnish with fat-free sour cream or plain yogurt.

Recipes for Tuesday

Corn lasagna
6 oz. skim mozzarella cheese, grated (1½ cups)
10 oz. pkg. frozen corn, thawed
15 oz. nonfat ricotta cheese
2 egg whites
1 lg. jar of Ragu spaghetti sauce (or make your own)
6 oz. lasagna noodles, uncooked
1 c. water

Preheat oven to 325 degrees. Spray 9 x 12 pan with Pam. In a medium bowl, combine 1 c. of the mozzarella, all of the corn, ricotta and egg whites. Line bottom of pan with 3/4 c. sauce. Layer half noodles, half cheese mixture, remaining noodles and remaining cheese mixture. Pour remaining sauce over the top. Carefully pour the water around the edges and sprinkle with the remaining mozzarella cheese. Tightly cover the pan with foil and bake for 1½ hours. Let stand for 20 minutes after baking. (This has only 5 gm. of fat per serving and is delicious!)

Cashew lettuce salad
head of green leaf lettuce, torn
1 c. Swiss (or favorite) cheese, grated
1 c. cashews (cashews tend to be high in fat; any nut will work)

If a recipe calls for oil in baked goods such as cakes and muffins, try using the same amount of applesauce instead.

1 red apple with peel on, chopped

Mix together and serve with poppy seed dressing or favorite dressing. (Use sparingly.)

Recipes for Wednesday

Cheesy Tuna (or Chicken) Bake
12 oz. noodles, cooked
11 oz. can of cheddar cheese soup
8 oz. fat-free sour cream
5 oz. skim evaporated milk
10 oz. broccoli (fresh or frozen, thawed)
12 oz. can of tuna in water (or 1 c. cooked chicken)
12 oz. pkg. shredded cheddar cheese
½ c. Parmesan cheese

Blend soup, sour cream and milk until smooth. Layer about 1 ½ cups of noodles, 1/3 c. tuna (or chicken), 1 c. broccoli and sprinkle with cheddar and Parmesan cheese in pan. Pour in 1 c. of sauce mix. Repeat layers and cover with remaining cheese.

Strawberry parfaits
1 pint fresh strawberries, quartered
3 T. brown sugar
1 T. granulated sugar
1 c. vanilla nonfat yogurt
¼ c. fat-free sour cream

In medium bowl, combine strawberries and sugars. Let stand about 20 minutes, stirring occasionally. In a small bowl, combine yogurt and sour cream. Spoon 1/3 berry mix into 4 parfait glasses, dividing evenly. Top each with 2 T. of yogurt mix. Repeat another layer. Top with remaining yogurt mix.

Recipe for Thursday

Stromboli
1 refrigerated can of Pillsbury french loaf
slices ham
sliced cheddar cheese (or your favorite)
raw vegetables (I use onions and green peppers)

Unfold the french loaf onto a greased (or sprayed) cookie sheet. Layer meat, cheese and vegetables. Wrap up edges and seal tightly. Bake at 350 until brown (about 18 minutes).

Recipe for Saturday

Orange Jell-O salad
large pkg. orange Jell-O
12 oz. Cool Whip
large can of chunk pineapple
2 large cans of mandarin oranges

Mix dry Jell-O and Cool Whip until smooth. Drain pineapple and oranges and add. Refrigerate for 2 hours.

We have leftovers about every three days so I schedule them on the menu calendar. So, if you count the two leftover days and the one day eating out, that leaves only four days of meal preparation! That's not so bad, is it?

Conclusion

Enough with the shame. We can eat real food that tastes great and satiates our tummies and our hearts. Stop the guilt and start making some small changes in the way you take care of yourself. Food is fuel and it is good for our bodies. It is fuel that will energize us and put us on the lifelong road toward health. By making wise choices and applying the W and the E of the WELL Principle to our everyday lives, we can eat without condemning ourselves. But good nutrition does require intentional planning or we're liable to fall into the diet dilemma, which is always a disaster.

Eating by the food pyramid and drinking plenty of good old-fashioned water leads to greater health and that influences our energy. Without adequate energy how can we possibly nurture relationships and keep our emotions in check? All that requires work. When we feel lousy because we're dehydrated and constantly dieting, being cheery, forgiving and encouraging is nearly impossible. We can take small steps—for example, start with four glasses of water a day and two servings of fruit each week—and work your way up to more.

Who knows? Like George Burns, we may live a long life and wish we'd done a better job taking care of ourselves.

Discussion Questions

1. How can you make a more concerted effort to drink more water? If you have more than two cups of caffeine a day, what will be the negative effect on your body?
2. Keep track of your food intake for a day. Are you getting the right amounts of carbs, protein and fat according to the Food Pyramid? How could you make better choices for nutrition?
3. Read Psalm 78:18. Are there certain foods that you crave that are not the healthiest choices? Why would this dishonor God?
4. Why must we be intentional in developing good eating habits? What are two habits from this chapter that you can begin to change?

Endnotes

1. Emilie Barnes and Sue Gregg, *Eating Right* (Eugene, OR: Harvest House Publishers, 1987), p. 127.
2. Pamela Smith and Carolyn Coats, *Alive and Well in the Fast Lane* (Nashville, TN: Thomas Nelson Publishers, 1993), pp. 68-69.
3. *Archives of Family Medicine*, Sept/Oct 2000.
4. *American Council on Exercise, Lifestyle and Weight Management Consultant Manual*, San Diego, CA, 1996, p. 96.
5. Smith and Coats, p. 24.
6. *Council Manual*, p. 193.

Chapter 8

Exercise: Developing the Heart Muscle

We couldn't wait to see the view from the top—and we weren't disappointed. Mike and I had just finished hiking up Diamond Head, the extinct volcano on the island of Oahu, and we were treated to a breathtaking panoramic view of the Pacific Ocean. With not a cloud in the sky, even Pearl Harbor several miles away was clearly visible along the palm tree coastline nestling Waikiki Beach. It was difficult to take in the magnitude of the splendor without using all of our senses. It was that overwhelming.

As beautiful as it was, I couldn't help wondering about the woman we had met while hiking up. We had been steadily progressing toward the top for about thirty-five minutes when the trail became markedly steeper and more rugged. Our pace slowed dramatically while our heart rates picked up steam. Fortunately we were both in fairly good physical condition so every few feet we would give each other a thumbs-up to say, "I'm OK. Let's keep going!"

After about five minutes of strenuous climbing, we were startled by a woman who was leaning against a rock, obviously overheated.

Her face was beet-red and her breathing was rapid and labored. She had been pushed beyond her limit and couldn't take one more step. We stopped immediately and asked her if she needed help. Between breaths, she assured us that she just needed a moment to calm down and catch her breath. We stayed with her until she could talk comfortably and her breathing and color were back to normal.

We offered to help her the rest of the way up but she declined. Then she said with solemn acceptance, "You kids go ahead. I guess I just wasn't prepared for how hard it was going to be. It looked so easy from the bottom. Somebody should post a warning sign down there about how hard it gets. Oh well, I sent my camera on up with the rest of my friends and they'll take plenty of pictures for me. Thanks for your help, though."

As I stood at the top and admired the glorious view, I remembered the woman who had struggled and how she would have only pictures to help her remember the beauty of Diamond Head. The look of disappointment on her face pained my own heart and I couldn't help but wonder how many other mountaintops she had missed.

Dear friend, that is exactly why we must never be too busy to exercise. If we don't keep our hearts strong we'll inevitably miss some of our own mountaintops. We won't have the endurance to press on when the going gets tough and we'll have to depend on others to help us recover. That is not God's best for us. His plan is for us to reflect strength and health, leading the way for others to follow our good example.

Are you leading others toward better health? Do people wonder why you have so much vitality and energy? Or do you feel guilty when exercise comes up in a conversation? Do you ever make excuses for why you're not exercising?

The truth is many people don't exercise because there is no impending doom glaring them in the face. They convince themselves they are healthy as long as they're not dead or in the hospital.

USA Today polled over 50,000 Americans to rate what they were most afraid of. Remembering that one out of four of us will die from heart disease, where do you think the fear of a heart attack was ranked? Probably number one? At least in the top ten?

It didn't even make the list! We are more afraid of not having enough money for retirement and being audited by the IRS than we are of having a heart attack, even though our chances are a hundred times greater!

One of my missions in life is to get so many people exercising that it puts my heart surgeon friend Tim out of business. When I remind him of this, he snickers and retorts rather confidently, "Laurie, that's never going to happen because we live in a self-indulgent country, and we've all convinced ourselves that heart attacks happen to the other guy (or gal)."

I know he's right, but I'll never stop trying.

Risk Factors

By now we should all know what increases our risk of a heart attack. But just in case we need a reminder, here's the list.

- *Genetics.* Because my dad died of his third heart attack at age fifty-two, I know I have a greater predisposition to it.

> Life is tons of discipline.
>
> *Robert Frost*

- *Age.* The older we are, the greater our chances.

- *Gender.* Men have more heart attacks at a younger age, but after menopause women and men are equal.

- *Smoking.* According to the American Cancer Society, cigarette smoke contains 4,000 chemicals, forty-three of which cause cancer. These chemicals include carbon monoxide, cyanide, formaldehyde and methanol. Smokers between the ages of thirty-five and seventy have death rates three times higher than those who have never smoked.

- *Hypertension.* High blood pressure is dangerous because it damages blood vessels and organs. Have you ever had the pressure too high in a garden hose when you water plants? With high blood pressure, the blood comes out of the heart with such force that it damages arteries and blood vessels, as well as our kidneys and liver.

- *Stress.* It should say quite enough that two entire chapters (4 and 5) of this book are devoted to the subject.

- *Sedentary lifestyle and obesity.* We don't move enough through the day so we are fatter than ever.

- *High cholesterol.* Too much fat in our diet.

Some risk factors we can't change, such as age, gender and genetics. But there are several that we can influence, and exercise is the best way.

The Rest of the WELL Principle

Because the heart is a muscle, it can be strengthened by exercise, aerobic exercise specifically. So the first "L" in WELL stands for Lift your heart rate. We need aerobic exercise because it increases the oxygen supply in the body which in turn increases metabolism. The higher our metabolism is (the rate at which we use calories), the easier it is to lose weight, maintain a healthy weight and reduce our risk of heart disease.

Benefits from aerobic exercise

Because a strong heart makes the rest of the body work more efficiently, there are many measurable benefits. The list is virtually inexhaustible, but here are several important ones.

- *More energy.* When we exercise, our bodies manufacture more red blood cells. The red blood cells carry iron, and iron carries oxygen. Where there are more red blood cells, there is more oxygen and therefore more energy.

- *Restful sleep.* People who exercise fall asleep faster and sleep more deeply because they have used up the extra adrenaline caused by stress. They feel more rested through the day and may be more productive than people who sleep longer but constantly toss and turn or wake up early.

- *Increases HDL Cholesterol.* Have you ever lived with a messy roommate? LDL cholesterol is like a messy roommate because it leaves "stuff" everywhere. In this case, the "stuff" is waxy fat that sticks to the blood vessels. HDL cholesterol is like the good roommate that goes around and picks up after all the messy people. This type of choles-

> The only way to change one's body weight is to begin a lifelong series of new habits.
>
> Dr. Jules Hirsh

terol helps keep the blood vessels clean.

- *Collateral circulation.* Fit people have bodies that can actually manufacture more blood vessels. If there is a blockage somewhere from plaque buildup and the blood can't get through the main arteries, collateral circulation allows the blood to take a detour and get back to the main road. (Isn't that amazing?)

- *Increased stroke volume.* Every beat of the heart is considered a "stroke," and the amount of blood the heart pushes out with each stroke is called volume. Stroke volume is the amount of blood pumped by each beat/stroke of the heart. The more blood the heart can pump, the better. People with strong hearts are able to reserve more energy because the heart can beat slower but do more work with each beat!

- *Ability to lose body fat.* One of the key ingredients to losing body fat is through aerobic exercise. It changes us inside so that our bodies work to make us lean. People who don't exercise have bodies that work to keep them fat—no kidding! We develop more enzymes that help fat be released from the fat cell when we exercise. The opposite is true when we don't. We develop enzymes that inhibit fat from being removed from the fat cell. That's why the fit get fitter and . . . you know the rest.

When Mindy came into the center to do some personal training with me, she was the classic profile of most of the people I train. At forty-two, she was fairly healthy (no injuries or apparent disease), about thirty pounds overweight (according to body fat percent, not the scale) and had developed some not-so-healthy eating habits (lots of fast food, no fruits or veggies).

She dabbled with exercise, jogging a mile or two when she had the time (once or twice a week). Mindy was already drinking plenty of water (like everybody else who succeeds here, she had her own special water bottle and carried it everywhere with her) but her eating needed some adjusting. She agreed to abide by the food pyramid guidelines, making wiser choices with her meals and snacks.

Eager to lose weight and feel more energized, she couldn't wait to start her program. That is, until I mentioned aerobic exercise. "You know, I really don't like to sweat," she informed me, hoping to persuade me to alter her plan. "I like to lift weights, but during aerobic activity I get so out of breath and my lungs feel like they are on fire. Can't I just do another day of weight training to make up for it?"

"I can understand why you wouldn't enjoy an activity like that. I'm not sure I would either." Thinking I was giving in, Mindy smiled and nodded her head, settling into her chair with a relaxed posture. But my statement was one of validation, not capitulation! "Mindy, let's take a minute to discuss what I mean by aerobic activity (a.k.a. cardiovascular training) because I think you'll be relieved to find out that you don't have to be miserable when you work your heart. I think we can find an activity that will be less strenuous and one that you will actually enjoy."

Budging ever so cautiously in my direction, she hesitantly asked, "OK, what did you have in mind?" Good. I was beginning to pique her curiosity.

"Mindy, do you know what 'aerobic' means?"

She thought for a moment, "Does it mean 'with air'? I think it has something to do with oxygen."

"That's exactly right. Aerobic exercise promotes the use and supply of oxygen in our bodies. That's why our breathing increases to the point where we need our mouths open for air."

"But that's what I don't like," Mindy reminded me. "I feel like I'm gasping for air."

"That's because you're actually working too hard," I assured her. "Here's the range I want you to be in: Work hard enough that you need your mouth open for extra air, but not so hard you can't carry on a conversation. That is called the 'talk test,' and it's a way for you to measure your intensity. You should feel the need to take a breath about every four or five words. But no gasping is necessary."

Mindy smiled, "Hey, I like that. Working and talking at the same time works for me!"

"Now, let's talk about how often you will exercise and how long each session will be. The fastest way to see results is to exercise five to six times a week, for a minimum of thirty to forty-five minutes." Some people are shocked that it is so often. They've always heard three days a week is enough. Mindy was no different.

"Why so often? That seems a little extreme, don't you think?"

"Our bodies respond best to things that are regular. If you exercise less than that you will still reap benefits, but they will be much slower in coming and you may get frustrated while you are waiting. In my twenty years of personal training I've had hundreds of clients successfully lose anywhere from ten to fifty pounds—and they all did it by exercising at least five days a week for about forty minutes.

"Besides that, the 1996 Surgeon General's report on health recommended thirty minutes every single day of the week for better health. Even the government confirms what I've been preaching! So, Mindy, it's really up to you. Do you want to exercise three days a week and see minimal results or do you want to see dramatic results ASAP?"

"Dramatic is good," Mindy agreed. "All right, you convinced me. How do I get started?"

Ah, music to my ears.

Mindy had just learned the principle of Frequency (how often we need to exercise), Intensity (how hard) and Duration (how long). She decided that she would start with five days a week for thirty minutes. The next step would be choosing the activity. Jogging was too intense for Mindy initially, so we started her on a more reasonable walking program. I knew she would see results that would be quick and permanent.

James Hill, a nutritionist at the University of Colorado at Denver studied more than 2,000 people who lost at least thirty pounds and kept them off for a year or more. These people, he says, share a commitment to exercise: they all walked forty-five minutes a day most days.[1]

Others back up Hill's discovery that however you drop pounds, walking is usually a key to

> Victory is not won in miles but in inches. Win a little now, hold your ground, and later win a little more.
>
> *Louis L'Amour*

staying slimmer. "It's highly unlikely you'll keep weight off if you don't increase your activity level," says James M. Rippe, a cardiologist at Tufts University School of Medicine, who has coauthored 120 papers on fitness. "For 95-plus percent of people, that means walking. It's simple, free, convenient and easy on the joints. And it burns lots of calories."[2]

For those intimidated by exercise and wanting to start as slowly as possible (far less than forty-five minutes every day), there is research to suggest you can do just that and reap some benefits. I-min Lee, an epidemiologist at Harvard, tracked 40,000 women age forty-five and older over a five-year period. Those who expended 200 to 600 calories a week walking (two to six miles a week) cut their odds of heart disease by an astonishing thirty percent. Women who had expended 600 to 1,500 calories a week (walking six to thirteen miles a week) saw their risk cut in half!

Lee discovered that even low levels of exercise in beginners produced gains in health, but "once you get in the exercise habit, upping the intensity of your workout can further help your heart. Bottom line: If you are just now pulling your long-lost walking shoes out of the closet, even a few easy rambles a week could save your life."[3]

The everyday commitment seems to be another key component for success since it eliminates the decision-making that can derail the best-intentioned exercise plans. We shouldn't give ourselves the option of missing our workout or we're just likely to take it. A tenacious attitude is part of the ingredient for success.

But no matter how much we exercise it does not give us license to eat with abandon. We must still apply the first two principles and continue drinking adequate water and eating by the food pyramid if we want to lose weight and increase our energy.

Some of the other benefits are that, according to Dr. Rippe, aerobic exercise seems to put a psychological brake on how much you eat. You get filled up faster and naturally take in fewer calories.

Yet another benefit is the calming effect on the brain. In one study Dr. Rippe conducted, he discovered a single forty-minute walk significantly lowered a person's level of anxiety and tension.[4]

At the University of Illinois at Urbana-Champaign in 1998, exercise psychologist Edward McAuley found that over a twenty-week period the participants in a walking program developed greater self-esteem, better body-image and increased self-worth. Such changes, he found, counteracted depression and anxiety.[5]

Apparently the best advice is that if you want to keep pounds off for good, stop starving yourself—and get moving.

Being in Illinois where the weather can vary forty degrees in one day, it was important for Mindy to have alternate plans for both indoor and outdoor activity. The other choices I gave her were:

Inside training

- Aerobic conditioning classes (the upbeat music makes the time go faster)
- Stationary bike/spinning classes (we can read at the same time for stationary biking; spinning classes are more intense)
- Elliptical machines (like cross-country skiing only smoother)
- Stepper (it's a great gluteal workout too)
- Racquetball or tennis (it's a social outlet as well)
- Treadmill (we can vary the degree of difficulty)
- Walking at a mall (shop at the same time!)

Outside training

- Walking/hiking (it's the number one aerobic exercise)
- Cycling (make it a family affair)
- Jogging (you'll get a runner's high)
- Mountain climbing (remember: safety first)
- Swimming (aqua-aerobics is easy on the joints)

The latest research from Brown University, presented at the 1999 meeting of the North American Association for the Study of Obesity, recommends daily moderate exercise for at least thirty minutes, with an hour being even better. They evaluated 2,500 people who lost an average of sixty pounds and kept it off, and found most exercised an hour most every day!

Obviously if you exercise that much and you do the same thing every day, it doesn't take long before you start to feel stale and a little bored. Here are some ways to spice up your workout.

- *Vary your route.* Try doing your familiar trek in reverse. Start where you usually finish.
- *Join a walking club.* It's great for motivation and companionship. You can call (800) AVA-WALK for a club near you.

> Nobody who ever gave their best regretted it.
>
> George Halas

- *Find a walking pal.* Most people need some kind of accountability to stay consistent. Have a different friend for each day if you like.
- *Listen to books on tape while you exercise.*
- *Sign up to walk a 5K or 10K event.*
- *Walk for charity.*
- *Walk backward for a while.* It will keep you alert.
- *Nature-walk.* Seek out routes blessed with woods, beaches or gardens.
- *Change your routine weekly.* Walk one week, bike the next, roller blade, jog, play tennis the others. Make up your own schedule or be spontaneous.

By cross-training and adding variety to our workouts, we protect ourselves from mental burnout. The more enjoyable we make exercise, the more likely it is we'll keep doing it.

Cautions for Pregnant Women

Mindy's children were grown, but there are some safety issues for those who are pregnant. Your blood volume increases a whopping thirty to fifty percent, heat production increases and hydration is critical. It is recommended that pregnant women keep their exercise low-impact, meaning their feet never leave the ground to jump. Hormones keep the ligaments loose during this time, so jarring from high-impact can cause the ligaments to lose their elasticity.

Also, when a pregnant woman's body temperature rises during exercise, so does the baby's. But while the mom can sweat to get cooled off, the baby can't. Be careful. The general rule is that during pregnancy your goal should be to maintain your fitness level (keep doing what your body is used to within reason) and wait until the baby is born to exercise more intensely.[6]

After four weeks on her walking program, Mindy voluntarily upped her time to forty minutes. She was becoming more comfortable with her conditioning program and had already lost six pounds! Not only that, she also reported feeling less tension through her shoulders and after years of restless sleep, she found that she would wake feeling completely rested and energized. She was heading in the right direction. How's your aerobic direction?

Aerobic exercise is our greatest weapon against heart disease. The truth is that we're not taking very good care of ourselves, and when life gets difficult, that wreaks havoc on our hearts. There are no warning signals to prepare us for rough road and our bodies break down from the stresses we face. Aerobic exercise helps prepare us for the journey. No one should ever have to miss the view from the top, and if we train our hearts aerobically, we'll never have to.

Why Get Pumped?

The last L in the WELL principle stands for Lift weights. Just as lifting our heart rate through aerobic exercise makes the heart stronger, lifting weights increases bone density, keeps joints strong and protected from injury and raises metabolism as well. "An increasing number of provocative studies indicates there's more to weight lifting than we suspected," says Barry Franklin, president of the American College of Sports Medicine.

For starters, stronger muscles make handling daily chores less of a strain, which relieves stress on the heart. And since muscle uses more calories than body fat does, we're less likely to become obese, a risk factor for heart disease. Lifting weights can also modestly lower bad LDL cholesterol levels. In the same vein, a recent analysis of eleven studies found that weight training eases blood pressure by a small but significant degree.[7]

David Grisaffi, a certified trainer and strength coach for three-time lightweight boxing champion Greg Haugen, explains why weight training is an important part of a successful fitness program. "It only takes three days of not working out before we begin deconditioning. On the average, a [somewhat sedentary] man in his mid-forties has already lost between ten and fourteen pounds of muscle, compared to a man in his mid-twenties. Thus, there is less muscle to burn off fat."[8]

As muscle tissue disappears, the body loses its efficiency in calling up stored fat for energy. And where a pound of fat needs only two calories a day to maintain itself, a pound of muscle (at rest!) needs an astonishing thirty-five to forty calories. "The thing to remember," he says, "is that every pound of lean muscle mass you gain will eat up to an additional 100 calories per day."[9]

Have you noticed men lose weight much faster than women? That's because men have more muscle than women and therefore a higher metabolism. Guys, this is a real advantage for you. When you exercise your body and eat healthy, nutritious foods, you can lose body fat fairly efficiently, certainly faster than most women, since we naturally have less muscle. But

> Healthy people don't dwell on past mistakes. They learn from their experiences and move on with new spirit and resolve.

you need to be even more careful to keep your body lean because most of the fat you carry is usually centered around your abdomen where all the major arteries that supply the heart with blood are located. That's why you have a greater predisposition to having a heart attack at an earlier age—your fat sits in a precarious position so close to the heart.

As a woman, I used to get upset that it was harder for us to lose fat. Now, I just accept the fact that I'm supposed to be "curvier" (euphemism for fatter), and I'm a whole lot happier. Plus, fat distributed in the hip and thigh area isn't so bad when you consider how much farther from the heart it is. Attitude is everything, girls.

Whether male or female, studies show that muscle can be gained in as little as six to eight weeks. Tufts University and the National Institute on Aging studied beginning weight trainers—ranging in age from seventy-five to ninety—and found that they averaged a ten percent increase in muscle mass and boosted their overall strength by more than 100 percent over a ten-week period.[10]

Wayne Wescott, the national YMCA's strength-training consultant, says, "Muscle is very active tissue. The advantage of strength training is that not only does it burn calories during and right after exercise (up to an hour after), it produces more muscle so you can burn more calories even while you are sleeping."

And that is a key component to losing weight because most of us can't possibly work out long enough during the day to burn thousands of calories. For a 150-pound person, the average calories used for an hour of walking are just 200.

For weight training, it's 270 (although weight workouts usually last far less time than that). Eating a meal while seated uses approximately ninety-three. Why is eating such a high calorie consumer? Most of the calories we use are not for movement, but to maintain our body temperature and functioning. The more muscle we have, the more calories we burn even when we are not moving.

How to pump it up

Mindy was comfortable with the idea of lifting weights because she had worked out in a gym years before. She expected me to pick up where her old trainer had left off in the mid-'80s, using very light weights and doing countless repetitions. She was quite surprised how much weight lifting had changed. When we sat down to go over her resistance training plan, I explained the new changes and why they would give her better results.

"Mindy, we are going to streamline your training so you can get your weights done in fifteen minutes. There's no need to do every machine anymore—besides, that would take an hour, and who has time for that?"

"Well I certainly don't. It would be great to be done in only fifteen minutes, but is that enough to make my muscles stronger?" she asked.

"Yes, you'll see quick results and it won't take all day to do it. I'll be giving you five different exercises, many of which train several muscles at the same time. You will be doing one set of each exercise with twelve to fifteen repetitions. The weight will be moderate in that you should be able to complete twelve repetitions with the last three being more of a struggle to finish. When you can do fifteen repetitions without really being challenged, it is time to make the weight heavier. Generally, we will add four to six pounds at that point. That is called progressive training and it is the fastest way to reshape and build your muscles."

"Wow, that doesn't sound so bad. Actually it sounds very doable. When can we start?"

That was four years ago and Mindy is stronger and leaner than she's ever been. She lost all of the thirty pounds she was hoping for and has muscle tone in places she didn't know had muscle.

I believe the best way to become fit, lose weight and successfully maintain a proper weight includes aerobic exercise *and* weight training. For some people that includes walking in the neighborhood and lifting weights at home on your own or with a video (I really like *The Firm* video series, anything by Kathy Smith and the low-impact video by Becky Tirabassi). For others, working out is best accomplished at a fitness facility like the YMCA or other fitness gyms. You may find it helpful to work with a trainer. Find someone who is knowledgeable and fits your personality. A good trainer will work with you and teach you how to make your workouts effective and safe. Plus it will make you accountable to someone and that will motivate you to keep going.

No spot-reducing

The only negative side to resistance training is that it doesn't miraculously take the fat off specific areas. For example, no matter how many sit-ups we do, we cannot remove an ounce of fat from the abdomen. That's because it is impossible to spot-reduce. Covert Baily, biochemist and best-selling author of *Fit or Fat*, says that we can

> Don't let what you can't do interfere with what you can.
>
> *John Wooden*

be sure spot-reducing doesn't work because if it did, people who chew gum or talk a lot would have skinny faces!

The most effective way to get started on a safe weightlifting program is to get professional instruction, either from a credible video or an experienced trainer. Look for the person with the greatest knowledge, not necessarily the one with the best body. Be savvy and investigate your options.

If you are just beginning and you want to purchase some weights for home, I would suggest three sets of hand weights for women: five pound, eight pound, ten pound. They usually come in sets and sell for around $15 a pair at Wal-mart or Target. For men, a little heavier is OK: ten-pound, twenty-pound, thirty-pound weights should be sufficient for beginners.

Conclusion

If we are to have a heart of energy by eating nutritiously and a stronger heart muscle by exercising aerobically, then we need to add only one thing to make it work—consistency. What we do day in and day out is truly what makes a difference. When we apply these principles consistently, our bodies accommodate the new habits we force upon them and they grow stronger. The human body is the only machine that actually breaks down when it is not used.

It is our daily habits that make or break the strength of our hearts. When we choose those habits wisely, we choose a heart of excellence.

Discussion Questions

1. Read First Timothy 4:8. How much value does physical training have in your life? Did exercise make the list for your top five pri-

orities? How could you include even thirty minutes in your daily schedule? Why does a healthy body honor God?
2. What barriers or obstacles prevented the success of previous attempts to get fit? What are some ways you can alleviate those?
3. Consider signing up for a new exercise program either at a club or YMCA or make up your own. Include some friends with common goals and commit to at least thirty minutes five days a week. What will be the rewards if you do this? What will be some of the sacrifices?

Endnotes

1. Nancy Bilyeau, *Lose Weight—Without Dieting*, a supplement to *Health Magazine*, 2000, p. 6.

2. Ibid., p. 7.

3. "Healthy News," *Health Magazine*, September 2000, p. 19.

4. Bilyeau, p. 10.

5. Ibid., p. 11.

6. Karen Redmond, M.S., Pre and Post Natal Training Guide, based on *American College of Obstetricians and Gynecologists: Exercise During Pregnancy and the Postpartum Period*, ACOG Bulletin #189, February 1994, n.p.

7. "Vital Signs: A New Reason to Get Pumped," *Health Magazine*, May 2000, p. 21.

8. Brian Leatart, *Prime Health and Fitness*, Fall 1997, p. 27.

9. Ibid.

10. Ibid., p. 28.

PART 4

SPIRITUAL

Chapter 9

Grace: With the Heart of a Father

Building deeper relationships, healing heavy emotions and developing stronger physical bodies lead us toward excellence and wholeness. Each part improves our quality of life and strengthens our hearts so we can find more fulfillment in everyday life. But the part of our lives that empowers us the most is our spiritual health. It is here that we come face-to-face with the wonderful truth that the God who created and sustains the entire universe knows us and loves us as His children. And His greatest desire is for us to know Him and love Him in return.

That's pretty amazing considering the state we are in. Let's face it: we're not an easy bunch to love. Even the best of us are judgmental, selfish, greedy, impatient, arrogant (shall I go on?). We're so bent on satisfying our own wants and needs that we have a hard time just getting along down here.

How could a perfect God long to love us when we are so wretched?

In a world that only gives standing ovations to an elite few, the idea of an omnipotent Creator and heavenly Father loving us unconditionally is foreign. That kind of love is difficult for many of us to believe because we weren't sure we were loved by our earthly fathers. If we were rejected and scorned by a dad who was like us, prone to sin, then how much greater the chance of being rejected by One who is perfect?

Painful memories

My father carried an overwhelming stress load and was an angry man most of the time. He worked long hours, often twelve or over, as a large-machine operator. He would come home completely exhausted but would continue working on projects around the house that needed repair, never resting or taking time for himself. Only work and more work.

There was kind of an unspoken "code of silence" around the house in the evening because we were afraid of upsetting Dad. But as the youngest and most rambunctious of five children, being quiet was especially difficult for me. I was vivacious and full of energy and life—always talking, laughing or yelling. But our house was small, which meant noise traveled quickly.

I knew when I had crossed the line because I could hear Dad's quick, heavy steps to find me. The look on his face would drive terror into my heart like a hammered nail into wood. Then he would swing his fists at whatever part of my body was closest to him while I screamed for him to stop. Sometimes he would use his belt or

> Forgiveness is our strongest weapon against ungrace.
>
> *Philip Yancey*

the metal end of the flyswatter to vent his rage, but usually his fists delivered the blows.

When I was only seven, I tried to run away. I packed my Barbie bag and hid behind the bushes in the backyard until they found me in the evening. I guess in my own childlike way I was trying to force my parents to say they wanted me, that I was loved as a precious daughter. I cried the whole time I waited for them to find me. I wanted so badly to belong to a family that cherished each other. And I wanted a daddy who would say, "Boy, am I glad you're my little girl."

God as Father

Donna Partow, best-selling author and speaker, shares a poignant story of longing to be daddy's girl. When Donna was a child she had a neighbor across the street who always called his daughter "princess." One day Donna asked her neighbor if she could be his princess too. He said, "No, you are *your* daddy's princess."

"Really?" Donna asked, surprised to hear the news.

"Of course," he said. "Just go ask your daddy. He'll tell you." You can imagine how fast Donna ran home. She burst into the room where her father was and asked, "Daddy, am I your little princess?"

He looked at her in stunned silence, then threw his head back and howled with laughter. "No! You're maggot mouth and leprosy legs!"[1] Those were his nicknames for Donna because her teeth had rotted down to stubs and her legs had so many mosquito bites they would swell and bleed.

Do you know the sting of your father's rejection? Is your heart heavy as you reflect on how your dad related to you? Longing to be treasured by your father crosses the gender line. Many men are also well acquainted with the heartache of their father's refusal to accept and esteem them, and they live their entire adult lives trying to measure up and prove them wrong.

Maybe you were blessed enough to grow up with a dad who validated your feelings and protected your emotions and well-being. In that case, you probably either wanted to be just like him or marry someone just like him.

Either way, your views of your heavenly Father are greatly influenced by the relationship you had (or have) with your earthly dad. But there is a greater reference point to explain just how good and tender and compassionate our heavenly Father is toward us.

The Word Is Truth

First John 3:1 says, "How great is the love the Father has lavished on us, that we should be called children of God! And that is what we are!"

All through the Bible, God uses phrases that help us understand the depths of His acceptance and esteem for us. Isaiah 49:16 reads, "See, I have engraved you on the palms of my hands." God loves us so much that He put our names in a place that He could see every moment of every day.

Another obstacle that keeps us from understanding God's incredible grace can come from growing up in a legalistic church that preaches you are saved by being "good."

I'll never forget the morning I was getting ready for church and a friend knocked on my door. It was Becky, a young, single gal who had grown up in church but had been walking a different road for the last couple years—trying to find love in all the wrong places, you might say. Surprised to see her so early (about 7 a.m.), the only thing that raced through my mind was either she desperately needed to borrow something or there must be some kind of an emergency. Turns out it was both.

I opened the door and Becky seemed eager to come in. "Laurie, please, I really need to talk. Can I come in for a little bit?" The anxious look on her face told me she needed more than "a little bit."

"Of course. Becky, what's wrong? Did something happen?" I half expected her to break down in tears. She obviously had something painful to tell me.

But she stayed composed as she unfolded her alarming story. "Laurie, I've been up all night partying and I didn't know where else to go."

"OK. But why aren't you home sleeping now? I would think you would be exhausted."

She laid it out for me in black and white. "Laurie, I can't sleep because I'm high on cocaine. Although I can tell I'm starting to come down, I just feel kind of numb. I can't even cry. All I know is I don't want to do this anymore, I just feel so out of control." She paused for a long time and I resisted the urge to fill dead air space with amateur counseling. Then she said, "I'll probably go to hell for this."

I decided church could wait and I made us some breakfast. I listened as she continued to share her journey from (as she referred to herself) "good Christian girl" before the drugs, to her current "sleazy, good-for-nothing loser." After a few hours she began to get tired and I suggested she sleep in our guest bedroom until she felt comfortable going home.

Becky slept for several hours until about dinner time, and when she awoke her emotions were no longer chemically suppressed. I heard

> It is to the prodigals . . . that the memory of their father's house comes back. If the son had lived economically he would never have thought of returning.
>
> *Simone Weil*

her gently crying at first, then weeping uncontrollably. When I knocked on the door to see if she was OK, she opened it to let me in. I held out my arms to comfort her (not sure if she was ready or willing to be comforted yet) and she cried on my shoulder for several minutes.

"What hurts the most, Becky?" I asked, doing my best to just listen rather than try to fix something I knew nothing about.

"Everything hurts. I feel so unlovable. I hate what I've become, I feel trashy. I'm afraid I'm so far from God I can never get back."

This I could help her with. "Becky, you can never be too far from God. He always wants you back. He can forgive anything!"

Not quite convinced, but seeming hopeful, Becky asked, "But isn't it unforgivable to turn your back on God after you become a Christian?"

Where in the world do people get this idea that they're only saved if they don't make mistakes? "Becky, we all turn our backs on God with our daily sin. Whether it's speaking ill of someone or being greedy or unforgiving, sin is sin. What you've been doing is no worse in God's eyes than when we refuse to be kind and loving to other people. I'm sure you know drugs are very dangerous to your body—even one experience with cocaine can cause sudden death—so we are going to get you some professional counseling to break the habit. Are you ready for that?"

Becky nodded with decision.

"But I don't think it's any accident that you came here today. You need to know that you are lovable—I love you, Becky. And God does too. It's His kindness that leads us to repentance (Romans 2:4). He never shames us when we fall—only people do that. He loves us back to Him. That's what grace is."

Becky cried again, only this time I knew it was because of the hope she felt.

Nothing we do can ever be bad enough to make God stop loving us. Somehow we have convinced ourselves that we must be perfect or at least better than average for God to be able to love us. That's wrong! While God is grieved when we make wrong choices and commit the same sins over and over, He will *never* take His love away. Isaiah 65:1-2 reinforces that where God says, "Here am I. Here am I. All day long I have held out my hands to an obstinate people." He holds His hands out, not as an angry father ready to strike a blow, but as a loving papa eager to hold and help the rebellious child he loves.

All you have to do to get a close-up look at God's grace is read the story of the prodigal son in Luke 15:11-32. When his wandering son started to make his way home after squandering his entire inheritance on wine and women, his father saw him while he was still a long way off. The father was so moved with compassion for him, "he ran to his son, threw his arms around him and kissed him" (15:20).

There was no solemn lecture, "I hope you learned your lesson!" Instead, there was exuberance so great that the father would publicly humiliate himself by rushing out to embrace a son that had just wasted half the family fortune.[2]

There is no greater force in all the earth than the love of your heavenly Father. Do you know that He finds you lovable? He longs to open His arms to you and welcome you back home—no matter what you've done.

Gift of Grace

So many Americans are giving up. Apparently many feel so unlovable and desperate that they're taking a permanent way out. Once every minute someone in the United States attempts suicide. Every day, seventy Americans take their own lives—that's nearly three each hour. In Los Angeles County, California, more people kill themselves than die in traffic accidents.[3]

> Sight and feelings are hindrances in believing and trusting God.
>
> Charles Stanley

Chuck Swindoll, from Insights for Living, says that the classic characteristic of a suicidal person is that they have a tragic sense of feeling unloved. By the looks of it, America has forgotten how to love.

If anyone were to feel unworthy of love, it should be Donna Partow. And yet I've had the privilege of speaking with Donna Partow at a women's conference and have heard the rest of her story. To meet her you would never dream how horribly she was treated, because today she is a radiant, attractive, confident woman of God. She has written several books and some excellent Bible studies. She knows firsthand the powerful and miraculous healing that can come from God's grace. She and her father enjoy a healthy and restored relationship. She who was once called unlovely beams with beauty.

Several weeks after Becky's Sunday morning visit, she showed up again. Only this time, it was to attend church with me. The pastor's sermon was on, of all things, "How to Find Your Way Back Home." He talked about the parable of the lost sheep in Luke 15:3-7 and how God will search high and low for a child that is lost. "Who of us, if we had a lost child in a store, would say it serves him right and just leave him to fend for himself?" Becky and I looked at each other and she leaned over and whispered, "Yeah, that's right. We wouldn't just leave him." I nodded in agreement.

"But because God is pure and holy," the pastor continued, "and we are sinners, we cannot have a relationship with Him unless we have some way to be pure and holy as well. God loves us so much that He sent Jesus who fit the description perfectly to save us and bring us back to the Father. Jesus paid for our sins by suffering through a horrendous death on the cross, reserved for the worst of criminals. He took the weight of our sins upon His back so that we could have a home—so we could live with our Dad."

When the pastor asked if anyone needed a home, my friend Becky went forward. She accepted Jesus as her Savior and Lord of her new life. She was finally free from the burden of "being good" and had a renewed hope that she was a much loved and lovely daughter.

Conclusion

Do you see how much God values being close to you? He sent Jesus from His right hand of glory to die a sinner's death, so that we could come home for all eternity.

Do you know Jesus as your Savior? Are you allowing Him to be Lord of everything in your life? Your strained relationships? Your damaged emotions? Your neglected physical health?

If you haven't accepted Jesus Christ as your Savior, you can do that right now. If you want God to forgive your sins, then you need to accept that Jesus Christ died for your sins, was buried and rose the third day, and that is how you are saved. Ask Him to be your Savior, and your heart will never be homeless again.

Discussion Questions

1. How have your previous experiences, either relationally or religiously, helped form your opinion of God?

2. Why do you think Paul was so quick to mention grace in all of his letters? What in your life, either past or present, is in need of grace?
3. Read Hebrews 4:16. Why does God sit on a "throne of grace"? How can we find grace in times of need?
4. According to Second Thessalonians 2:16-17, what is the purpose of grace? How have you seen that demonstrated either in your life or the lives of others?

Endnotes

1. Donna Partow, *Becoming a Vessel God Can Use* (Minneapolis: Bethany House Publishing, 1996), pp. 92-93.

2. Philip Yancey, *What's So Amazing About Grace?* (Grand Rapids, MI: Zondervan Publishing House, 1997), p. 52.

3. Charles R. Swindoll, *Come Before Winter* (Portland, OR: Multnomah Press, 1985), p. 95.

Chapter 10

Discipline: Following Wholeheartedly

"David! What are you doing? Are you nuts? You can't go out there—you'll be killed!"

Can you just imagine David's brothers shouting at him to stay away from Goliath as they huddled a safe distance away? They probably wondered, *What on earth can he be thinking? He's just a small, insignificant shepherd boy sent to check on us as we help fight against the Philistines. And now he's marching out there to do battle with a nine-foot giant, whose name alone sends terror to the heart of all Israel, with some rocks and a sling. Get real, David.*

I have to admit I would have been right there yelling and hiding with his brothers. Does it make sense to you? This little boy who works with sheep because he's low man on the totem pole is now going to slay a giant who has a coat of armor weighing 125 pounds and a spear whose pointed end weighs fifteen pounds? Right. It would take a miracle for that to happen. . . .

But then, God specializes in using the most unlikely people to bring about the most incredible results.

> Your biggest weakness is God's greatest opportunity.

What about shy Moses with a speech impediment? He reminded God at least six times that he couldn't speak, believing that God had the wrong man for the job. But Moses led more than a million Israelites out of Egypt, crossed the Red Sea and became the only man who knew the Lord face-to-face (Deuteronomy 34:10).

Gideon was from the weakest family in their clan and he was considered the least in his family. Talk about a self-esteem boost! Yet God used him and only 300 soldiers to save his people from 120,000 Midianites.

At first glance, David, Moses and Gideon are unlikely heroes for anything, much less saving a nation. But that is exactly what they did because they followed God wholeheartedly.

When we believe that God loves us as a Father and that Jesus Christ was sent to redeem us, the next step is learning how to obey. Jesus said in Matthew 22:37 that the greatest commandment is to "love the Lord your God with all your heart and with all your soul and with all your mind."

To love God more than anything else in this world, to have that as the top priority in our lives, to choose actions and develop habits that demonstrate that commitment is to follow God wholeheartedly. When we do, God will begin using us, the most unlikely of heroes, to reach out to a hurting world and show them His saving grace.

After my friend Becky accepted Christ as her personal Savior (even though she grew up in church, she wasn't sure if she had ever done that), we had many conversations about the next step. "I just don't want to mess up anymore, Laurie," she said. "I've made so many mistakes that have hurt a lot of people. I don't ever want to do those things again. I want to live a pure life. What can I do to change?"

"Becky, what I've learned about obedience is simple enough to put into four words: *Stay close to Him*! I can say without exception that when I struggle with sin—whether it's lust, spending too much money, envying my neighbor or being impatient with others—it is because I try to handle things on my own and I don't include God in my day."

Becky looked surprised and asked, "You struggle with sin?"

"Yeah—no matter how long you've been a Christian, there are times when it's the hardest thing in the world. A few years ago, I felt like I was going through a dry time spiritually. I felt alone and depressed. I felt like the biggest failure as a Christian and I just couldn't even bring myself to pray. This went on for months. Then when I was at a women's conference, the speaker was talking about Jesus, the gentle Shepherd, and how He loved me just the way I was. I could feel my heart begin to soften at the thought. Then I remembered how a shepherd would teach one of his sheep not to stray. He would break its leg."

"On purpose?" Becky asked with disbelief.

"Yes, on purpose."

"Ouch, that must have hurt. Why in the world would he do that? It seems cruel."

"He did it so the sheep couldn't wander away where it could be killed or hurt by another animal. He carried the sheep for several weeks while its leg was healing. During that time, the sheep was close to the shepherd's voice and learned to recognize it better. Also

> It is not enough for me that God has given me grace once, but He must give it always. I ask that I may receive; and when I have received, I ask again. The more I drink, the more thirsty I become.
>
> *Jerome*

I imagine that the shepherd rubbed the sheep's back and stroked its neck, increasing the sheep's dependence on him. That would keep the sheep from straying when it could walk again."

"Wow, so it was actually a good thing because it kept the sheep safer in the end," Becky surmised.

"That's right. And I thought about all of that while I was sitting in the conference and I finally prayed, *Lord, help me. I don't know how to get back to You. Lord, break my leg.*"

"Oh my goodness," Becky interrupted, "that was courageous. So, did He?"

I laughed as I imagined God literally doing that in the middle of a conference and the mass exodus that would ensue when the other attendees took notice. "What I meant when I said that to Him was *God, do what it takes to bring me back to You, even if it hurts.* And do you know, Becky, when I prayed that, I was filled with a sense of compassion from God. It softened my heart even more, so I asked Him what was wrong with me. I thought I would hear a long list of sins but I only heard one word: neglect."

I told Becky how I had been neglecting God. He reminded me of a scripture I had memorized—Jeremiah 2:13—that says, "My people have committed two sins: They have forsaken me, the spring of living water, and have dug their own cisterns, broken cisterns that cannot hold water." He was telling me that all my bad deci-

Discipline: Following Wholeheartedly

sions were rooted in my first sin, neglecting Him. Not spending time in His presence through prayer, not reading His Word or memorizing it. Not seeking Him or thinking about Him or dwelling on His goodness. I was giving lip service to my halfhearted Christianity and it caused all the other sins I was struggling with.

"Oh, Laurie, How do we stay close to Him? I don't want to be halfhearted either," Becky said. "What can we do?"

"Fortunately God didn't leave that to chance," I reassured her. "He didn't just say, 'Love Me with all your heart, mind and soul' and then leave us to figure it out on our own. He left us a manual with all the 'how-tos' in black and white. He makes it clear through Scripture what He wants us to do."

"Do you know where to find that? Growing up in the church, I should know my Bible better, but honestly I've never read more than a few paragraphs here and there. I'm anxious to learn all I can."

"You know, Becky, the problem with me is that I do know what God says. I just often say no."

Becky smiled with understanding but I was glad she didn't let me off the hook by saying something like, "I'm sure God understands."

"The truth was," I continued, "I knew He wanted me to be more obedient."

> Those who imagine they can attain holiness by any wisdom or strength of their own will find themselves, after many labors and struggles and weary efforts, only farther from possessing it.
>
> *John of Avila (1502-1569)*

Becky patted my hand and said, "Maybe we can help each other."

I appreciated her honest encouragement. "You know, Beck, if I had to narrow it down to four principles that were essential to living in obedience and following God wholeheartedly, I would say: *Reading the Bible, memorizing Scripture, praying, loving others.*"

"Am I supposed to do all four at the same time?" Becky asked.

"Yeah, but you can start small, spending maybe fifteen minutes a day with the first three, then increasing your time when you're ready. After seven years of doing this, I like to spend an hour, but start where you are comfortable. Loving others is what we want to do more and more when we spend time reading and praying. Loving is the natural progression of learning."

"OK, that makes sense. Keep going, I'm with you."

"A couple of verses that encourage and command us to be in God's Word are Psalm 119:2, that says, 'Blessed are they who keep his statutes and seek him with all their heart.' Verses 9-11 continue with instruction: 'How can a young man keep his way pure? By living according to your word. I seek you with all my heart; do not let me stray from your commands. I have hidden your word in my heart that I might not sin against you.'

"Scripture makes it clear, Becky, that to know God we must spend time in His Word. I have found what works best for me is to read two chapters a day (you can start with any book, although beginning in Genesis has been helpful to me) and then write in a journal what it means and what can be learned from it. It makes it easier to remember and apply to everyday situations when it's written down."

Becky agreed. "Yeah. What good is it to read it if I'm not going to be changed by it?"

It was exciting to be sharing what I had learned (at least in my head) with someone so anxious to absorb it. I told her that to "hide His Word" means we need to memorize it so that it will keep us from sinning. The entire chapter of Psalm 119 is about the importance of reading God's Word and how it is the best way to seek Him and stay pure. I had started with one Scripture a month. That way I knew I could have success and that would make it fun, not frustrating.

The very first one I ever memorized was Second Timothy 1:7: "For God did not give us a spirit of timidity, but a spirit of power [boldness for Him], of love and of self-discipline." I've memorized on my own and with friends, and it's definitely easier to make yourself do it when you are accountable to someone.

"We could do that, couldn't we?" Becky responded. "I mean, if I can memorize the words to my favorite songs on the radio and TV jingles for Pete's sake, I think I could memorize one Scripture a month."

She was right!

"Next," I continued, "we are to pray. First Thessalonians 5:17 says that we are to 'pray continually.' There is no mystery to prayer. It is simply talking to our heavenly Father, and then being quiet enough to give Him a chance to respond. Some people like to use the acronym ACTS to have some order to how they pray. The A stands for adore, C for confession, T for thanksgiving and S for supplication (requests). Have you heard of these?"

"I think so, but why don't you explain it and I'll try to remember it this time."

> Periods of staleness in the life are not inevitable but they are common.... In short, we can keep from going stale by getting proper rest, by practicing complete candor in prayer, by introducing variety into our lives, by heeding God's call to move onward and by exercising quiet faith always.
>
> *A.W. Tozer*

Adoration

Adoration can be difficult to learn because it is something we do for God for the sole reason of worshiping Him. We're not asking for anything, and we're not telling Him about a sin. We are reveling in who He is, and that takes practice. You know, the world gives incredible adulation and praise to great athletes like Michael Jordan, Tiger Woods and Mark Maguire, but they can't save a soul. They almost defy humanness, yet can they grant eternal life to anyone, including themselves? It won't be long until these gentlemen, as amazing as they are, will be too old to play basketball, too decrepit to swing a club and too worn out to swing a bat. Their athletic magic will one day be a memory and their records broken by the next superstar.

But God is the same yesterday, today and tomorrow. He doesn't change. He is as strong as the day He made the world and as compassionate as when He sent Moses to deliver His people. God will never become too old, tired or out of shape—He's perfect! If anybody deserves adoration, it's God!

"But wouldn't it be enough to worship Him at church?" Becky asked.

"Well, let me ask you—is once a week enough for you to hear how wonderful you are? Or would every day be better?"

Becky laughed. "Hey, I'll take it any way I can get it, but if I had to choose—yeah, I'd want to hear it every day if I could."

There are so many different ways to praise God. My personal favorite is through music. I grew up in a traditional Christian church which sang the classic hymns like "How Great Thou Art," "Amazing Grace" and "Nearer to Thee." While I greatly enjoy singing and listening to contemporary choruses, there is something so rich and meaningful about singing the songs I learned as a child. I keep an old hymnbook next to my Bible and journal and frequently glance through the pages, reading the powerful words to songs that were penned hundreds of years ago but are still relevant today.

Confession

The "C" in ACTS stands for confession. Confessing our sins is a lot like having a splinter removed. It can really sting but there is immediate relief when it is out. If the splinter is deep, it can be a slow and painful process. But the alternative is worse. Allowing a splinter to remain in the skin only invites infection and perpetuates the pain.

Unconfessed sin separates us from God. But when we admit it, it keeps our prayers from being hindered. Psalm 66:18 says, "If I had cherished sin in my heart, the Lord would not have listened." In Psalm 32:3-5, David says,

> When I kept silent,
>   my bones wasted away
>   through my groaning all day long.
> For day and night
>   your hand was heavy upon me;
> my strength was sapped
>   as in the heat of summer.
> Then I acknowledged my sin to you
>   and did not cover up my iniquity.
> I said, "I will confess
>   my transgressions to the LORD"—
> and you forgave
>   the guilt of my sin.

"Now, David was a man who knew sin. Can you believe he actually had a man killed so he could keep sleeping with that guy's wife?" Becky interjected. "I guess David's life was about as scandalous as mine. God's ears sure get filled with a lot of terrible confessions."

> I've never been surprised by God's judgment, but I'm still stunned by His grace.
>
> Max Lucado

"Yeah, but Becky, that's why Christ died—to save us from ourselves. God knows everything we've done, but He waits for us to tell Him we're sorry so we can be free from it and learn to stop doing it. Whatever 'it' is. You know what I love about God? He never forgets our sin. I mean, He can't forget—He's perfect. But He *chooses not to remember!* Hebrews 8:12 says, 'For I will forgive their wickedness and will remember their sins no more.'"

The confession part of our prayer time, even though painful at times, will have a profound effect on our character. It frees us emotionally because the guilt is gone. It makes us want to forgive others because we ourselves have received undeserved mercy. And it draws God nearer to us because He longs to comfort a repentant heart (Psalm 34:18).

God's forgiveness cleanses our hearts and His mercy teaches us to fear Him. When we have a reverent respect for God and His Word, it will keep us from asserting our own will in disobedience. We'll sin less because we love Him more.

How to confess

The best way to confess your sins to God is to name them specifically. When we pray a blanket prayer over them and don't call them by name, we are not forced to face exactly what they are. They must be exposed to the refiner's fire so they are not kept as secrets in our hearts, taking root and growing deeper.

Rather than saying, "Lord, please forgive me for my sins today," it prunes our character more effectively when we can say, "Lord, I'm sorry I was selfish when I didn't pitch in at the church during the cleanup time. I was standing right there when they asked for help, but I turned my back because I wanted to get home and relax. I'm sorry I didn't give them even a few minutes of my time." That identifies the root of the problem—selfishness. When I admit what the real sin is, I can work on getting rid of it. It helps me recognize my tendencies to sin and gives me clearer direction for how to act next time.

We need to confess the sin to the Lord specifically, and sometimes we need to confess it to the person we're angry with. James 5:16 reads, "Therefore confess your sins to each other and pray for each other so that you may be healed."

If someone has hurt you or offended you and you harbor resentment against him, that is just as bad as what he has done to you! How can your heart be pure if you burn with anger against someone you are commanded to forgive? Sometimes the only way to break free of this bitterness is to confess your sin to the person and ask forgiveness. Even if he has not apologized for hurting you, you are still responsible for keeping your own heart pure—and that is not my suggestion, but God's command.

Thanksgiving

After we confess our sins, our hearts are freer to enjoy an intimate time of conversation with the Lord. This is a great time to thank Him for all of the blessings in your life. It's amazing how grateful we feel when we acknowledge all the good in our lives. Filling our hearts with thankfulness keeps us from complaining and being discontented.

"Laurie, I never knew that God purposely doesn't remember my sins anymore!" Becky exclaimed. "That is so comforting and at the same time it helps me see Him as a loving father rather than a big ogre that is keeping all my sins in some big book somewhere—and in my case, a very big book."

"That's why confession leads right into thanksgiving. We want God to have the glory for the good things in our lives."

When we thank God for our blessings, we are acknowledging that He is the source, which keeps us from puffing ourselves up and accepting the credit.

This was a painful lesson for our family the summer of 1995. At the time, Mike was a golf course superintendent at a country club. The grass had been beautiful all spring and summer, and honestly, we believed it was a result of Mike's expertise and extensive knowledge. He had been recognized with positions of authority on the board of directors for superintendents and had received many accolades among his peers and club members. In August, the weather turned nasty, staying hot and humid even at night when the grass needs cool temperatures in order to recover from the heat stress. Mike checked the course constantly for any sign of disease.

On Saturday morning, August 12, Mike spent an inordinate amount of time checking the grass, knowing those were prime conditions for a disease that could wipe the course out in a matter of hours. Every inch of the course was in good shape—healthy, in fact. I applauded him for being such a genius.

By 4 o'clock that afternoon, seventy-five percent of the course was diseased and dying. He called his crew in immediately and they worked into the night trying to save as much grass as possible, to no avail. The course had to close for two months while they worked on an extensive recovery program.

That taught us a great deal about taking credit for God's blessing. We've learned to thank Him for His goodness, giving Him the glory and reminding ourselves that every good and perfect gift comes from His hand, not ours.

"Laurie, what do you think of Oprah's idea? Every day she writes a list of ten things she's thankful for that have blessed her."

"I think that it's a good idea to write down our blessings—remembering they're from God!—because we have very short memories. I've looked back over some of my journals and have been amazed at all the blessings I'd forgotten about, but seeing them in my journal brought them back to my memory. Also, I use that part of my journal to thank God for the answered prayers He's provided."

"Yeah, I'm gonna do that too. Is that how you keep track of what you have to pray for? In your journal?"

"Yes, and now when people ask me to pray for them I actually remember to do it."

Supplication

Of all the disciplines in the ACTS, supplication is the one we are most familiar with because this world is so needy. That need may be from a sickness, death in the family, job loss, car accident, depression, broken relationships, confusion, addiction—the list is endless. But what is

> Give thanks to the LORD, for he is good. His love endures forever.
>
> *Psalm 136:1*

the same is that we want to know there is a higher Power in charge that can run to our rescue.

I remember being moved to tears as I watched the CNN coverage on Walter Payton's emotional plea for America to pray for him as he waited for a liver donor. He died a few months later and we lost someone whose nickname depicted his character as well as athletic ability—"Sweetness." It's almost impossible to watch any tragic news story without hearing someone's request for prayer.

C.S. Lewis said, "Pain is God's megaphone to get the attention of our hearts." Life is so full of pain—we must be awfully hard of hearing.

God tells us over and over again that we can come to Him with our problems. He wants to help us. It's His nature as a loving Father.

He commands us to ask

- First Peter 5:7: "Cast all your anxiety on him because he cares for you."
- James 4:2: "You do not have, because you do not ask God."
- Hebrews 4:16, "Let us then approach the throne of grace with confidence, so that we may receive mercy and find grace to help us in our time of need."

God wants us to pray about everything in our lives because He wants to be involved. But He doesn't force His way in; He waits to be invited. We show Him that we are open to His guidance by asking for His intervention. By asking for help, we are proving how much we depend on Him and that pleases Him. It is our arrogance and pride that push Him away.

How's your communication with the Lord? Have you told Him what is bothering you or causing you anxiety lately? Or are you trying to brave it alone? God doesn't say to pray about a problem only if it's keeping you up at night, or if it has significant value for at least five other people. If it is important enough for you to think about, God wants to hear it!

The year the grass died on the golf course was also the year we celebrated our ten-year anniversary on September 28th. I knew God cared about strengthening our marriage, so I asked God to send us someplace special for our anniversary. I had always wanted to go to Hawaii, but that wasn't going to be financially possible outside of some miracle, so I told the Lord wherever it was, I would be grateful.

A week later, I received a phone call from a friend who knew nothing about our tenth anniversary or my prayer. And she said, "Laurie, we're not going to be able to use our time share this fall and we wondered if you and Mike could use it. We don't want any money for it because it will just be wasted if no one can use it. It's in Mexico, but you can trade it for almost anywhere in the world."

Think that was a fluke? We spent our ten-year anniversary in Hawaii—for free! We had enough frequent flyer miles for one ticket and a generous friend gave us the other and several hundred dollars to take with us!

See? Nothing is too small or insignificant for God to care about. When I shared that amazing story with a casual friend, she told me I had

> If you want to have faith that can move a mountain, then keep your eyes not on the mountain, but on the Mountain-mover.

> Nothing will motivate you to pray like seeing your prayers answered. They may not be in the way you want, but they will be in the way you most need.

better not pray like that very often because I might use up God's goodness and take it away from someone who really needs it. I thought that comment was humorous at first, but then I realized how sad it must be to think of God as stingy. That friend saw God as a small god with limited blessings and thin patience—but friends, it is a compliment to God to ask Him to do miracles. He loves to pour out His blessings, and He has an infinite supply!

God wants you to bring every request to Him, so that He can sift it through His hand of love and give you back what is best for you. That doesn't always mean the pain or the problem will instantly disappear, but it does mean that He will guide you through it, perhaps allowing you to face adversity to strengthen your faith.

Do you trust Him with all that you have?

A plan for prayer

"Laurie, you seem to know God's Word pretty well," Becky told me. "So, if you don't mind me asking, what led to your spiritually low time when you were at the conference, you know, with the broken leg and all?"

I respected her honesty. "Becky, my plan has been the same for years and years, and that is to pray constantly, about everything. To do that, I schedule it on my DayTimer. That is usually first thing in the morning, after Mike has gone to work and before the phone starts ringing.

Discipline: Following Wholeheartedly

"I always sit at the kitchen table as I read and journal, because I'm less likely to fall asleep there. Having the same 'meeting' place helps establish a habit and I think that place somehow becomes holy with His constant presence. I read and then I journal what I want to remember from the passage. I reflect on the blessings from the previous day and I enter those in my journal. After that, I enter the specific prayer requests for particular days (Pastor on Sunday; teachers on Tuesday, etc.).

"Then I move to the family room so I can play music and begin moving through the ACTS. First I adore the Lord and sing praises to Him. Then I confess the specific sins I've committed and ask God to reveal any I may not be honest enough to admit. After confessing my mistakes and allowing the splinters to be removed, I give thanks for all God is doing in my life. Finally, I lift up all the requests to Him to be taken off my shoulders and onto His."

"That sounds great, Laurie. So how did you become so dry if you were doing all that?"

"Simple. I stopped doing it."

"Well, why did you stop when you knew better?" (Everybody should have such a forthright friend!)

"I stopped because one day I let the urgent things come before the important. It's not that I ever said, *I'm just not going to read today* or *Boy, I'm too busy to pray*. I always intended to get to it. In the back of my mind I was saying, *I'll do it in an hour or just a little bit later. I'll get to it after one more phone call, one more errand.* But it just kept getting put off and before I knew it several weeks went by and then months. By then I needed more than a splinter removed, I needed major surgery."

"And now? Are you doing any better?"

"My friend Lynn told me that to establish a habit you have to approach it like an alcoholic does with sobriety. You can't fall off the wagon because then the habit will not be established and old patterns take over. Although alcoholics should *never* take another drink, she suggested not allowing myself to miss a day for two months. By then I would have what psychologists refer to as 'habit strength' and it would become more automatic. It was really helpful for me to look at it in those terms, that establishing the habit was the first step to being able to stick with it."

"Wow, that's a good lesson for me too. I tend to give up on anything that requires discipline," Becky admitted sheepishly.

How about you? Are you tired of carrying the world on your shoulders? Feel guilty that you're not consistent with your praying? Why don't you let the One who was strong enough to carry the weight of our sins to the cross help lighten your load?

"OK, so now the really hard question," Becky said. "How do I do a better job loving people? Laurie, there are people I can't stand to be around. Maybe I should start with 'liking' and work up to 'loving,' do you think?"

"I know that encouragement is very important and makes people feel loved. When I was hard pressed one week to finish a writing deadline, my friends Nancy and Rebecca showed up with a box of goodies, juice, hard candy, crackers, gum, cookies and a card that several people had signed to say, 'You can do it.' That was so special. I was able to stay up later than I had planned that night to finish the project on time because they had encouraged me (and gotten others to as well).

"Investing time is also a good one. I remember when my friend Suzi showed up one day to help me clean my house when we were getting ready to sell it. That made me feel loved. And it's important to give our resources, whether that's money or time. God wants us to be extremely generous with both. People feel loved when we share. How about you? What makes you feel loved, Becky?"

Discipline: Following Wholeheartedly

She looked serious for a moment, as if trying to recall something from her past. Then her countenance softened. She gently smiled and whispered, "Grace."

> Let us then approach the throne of grace with confidence, so that we may receive mercy and find grace to help us in our time of need. (Hebrews 4:16)

Discussion Questions

1. What are some characteristics about God that you love? Take a moment and tell God how wonderful He is and what you appreciate about Him.
2. Do you have any unresolved conflicts with others that could hinder your prayers? Take a moment and confess your sins to God. Ask Him to reveal any that you might not be aware of or are being too stubborn to admit.
3. Make a list of things you are thankful for. They can be relationships, your profession, material provisions, etc.
4. For each day of the week, write down the name of a person who needs your prayers. Make it a goal to pray for that person for two minutes on that day. At the end of the year you will have prayed for that person for almost two hours!

Once you were alienated from God . . . because of your evil behavior. But now he has reconciled you by Christ's physical body through death to present you holy in his sight, without blemish and free from accusation.

Colossians 1:21-22

5. Read Psalm 1:1-3. What does God instruct us to do? How often? What does He promise accordingly?

Recommended Reading

Relational: Marriage

Kay Arthur, *A Marriage Without Regrets,* Eugene, OR: Harvest House Publishers, 2000.

Gary Chapman, *The Five Love Languages,* Chicago: Northfield Publishing, 1995.

James Dobson, *What Wives Wish Their Husbands Knew About Women,* Wheaton: Tyndale Publishing, 1975.

Willard F. Harley, Jr., *His Needs, Her Needs,* Grand Rapids, MI: Fleming H. Revell, 1994.

Cynthia Heald, *Loving Your Husband,* Colorado Springs, CO: NavPress Publishing Group, 1989.

Mike Mason, *The Mystery of Marriage,* Sisters, OR: Multnomah Books, 1985.

Stormie Omartian, *The Power of a Praying Wife,* Eugene, OR: Harvest House, 2000.

Relational: Parenting

Steve Farrar, *Point Man—How a Man Can Lead His Family,* Sisters, OR: Multnomah Books, 1990.

Josh McDowell and Dick Day, *How to Be a Hero to Your Kids,* Dallas: Word Publishing, 1991.

Stormie Omartian, *The Power of a Praying Parent,* Eugene, OR: Harvest House, 1995.

Rick Osborne, *Teaching Your Child How to Pray,* Chicago: Moody Press, 2000.

Joe White, *What Kids Wish Parents Knew About Parenting,* West Monroe, LA: Howard Publishing Company, Inc., 1998.

Emotional

Dr. Henry Cloud and Dr. John Townsend, *Boundaries,* Grand Rapids, MI: Zondervan Publishing House, 1992.

Dr. Archibald D. Hart, *Adrenaline and Stress,* Dallas: Word Publishing, 1995.

Jean Lush, *Women and Stress,* Grand Rapids, MI: Fleming H. Revell, 1992.

Charles Stanley, *How to Handle Adversity,* Nashville, TN: Oliver-Nelson Books, 1989.

Richard A. Swenson, M.D., *The Overload Syndrome,* Colorado Springs, CO: NavPress Publishing Group, 1998.

Physical

Covert Bailey, *The Ultimate Fit or Fat,* Boston: Houghton Mifflin Company, 1999.

Nancy Clark, *Sports Nutrition Guidebook,* Champaign, IL: Human Kinetics, 1997. (Not just for athletes!)

Kenneth Cooper, *Faith-based Fitness*, Nashville, TN: Thomas Nelson Publishers, 1995.

Kenneth Cooper, *Regaining the Power of Youth at Any Age*, Nashville, TN: Thomas Nelson Publishers, 1998.

Heather Harpham Kopp, *The Dieter's Prayer Book*, Colorado Springs, CO: Wahterbrook Press, 2000.

Pamela Smith, *Food for Life*, Lake Mary, FL: Creation House, 1994.

Spiritual

Charles Colson, *How Now Shall We Live*, Wheaton, IL: Tyndale House Publishers, 1999.

Bill Hybels, *Too Busy Not to Pray*, Downers Grove, IL: InterVarsity Press, 1988, 1998.

C.S. Lewis, *Mere Christianity*, New York: Macmillan, 1976.

Max Lucado, *In the Grip of Grace*, Dallas: Word Publishing, 1996.

John Piper, *Desiring God*, Sisters, OR: Multnomah Books, 1996.

Philip Yancey, *What's So Amazing About Grace?*, Grand Rapids, MI: Zondervan Publishing House, 1997.

For women
Donna Partow, *Becoming a Vessel God Can Use*, Minneapolis, MN: Bethany House Publishers, 1996.

For men
R. Kent Hughes, *Disciplines of a Godly Man*, Wheaton, IL: Crossway Books, 1991.

To contact Laurie about a speaking engagement, write to her at:

P.O. Box 279
Savoy, IL 61874

or call CLASS at
1-800-433-6633